Caring for the Sick and Elderly

A Parish Guide

SR. MARIE ROCCAPRIORE, MPF

CARING
for the SICK *and*
ELDERLY
A PARISH GUIDE

TWENTY-THIRD PUBLICATIONS
185 WILLOW STREET • PO BOX 180 • MYSTIC, CT 06355
TEL: 1-800-321-0411 • FAX: 1-800-572-0788
E-MAIL: ttpubs@aol.com • www.twentythirdpublications.com
Bayard

Twenty-Third Publications
A Division of Bayard
185 Willow Street
P.O. Box 180
Mystic, CT 06355
(860) 536-2611 or (800) 321-0411
www.twentythirdpublications.com
ISBN:1-58595-249-4

Library of Congress Catalog Card Number: 2002111931
Printed in the U.S.A.

Dedication

To God
in praise and thanksgiving
for the blessed years spent caring for my Mom.

To the Sisters in my community, the Religious Teachers Filippini,
particularly those who care for the Sisters in the infirmary at Villa Walsh,
or who minister to the sick and elderly in their families or parishes

In Grateful Acknowledgment

To my parents, Josephine and Vitaliano Roccapriore, who taught me true reverence and respect for the sick and elderly by their words, example, and inspiration. May they now enjoy eternal rest in heaven!

To my sisters-in-law and to my brothers, Frank, Joe, Gerry, Richie, Vic, and Vito, for their loving encouragement and support.

To Sue and Mark Hallbach, and Frankie and Carl Carron, for inspiring me with their patience and unwavering faith during their young sons' battle with cancer and eventual death. It was a privilege to have been able to bring Eucharist to Mark and Kevin. They brought me some of life's treasured moments.

To Fr. Robert Rousseau, Fr. Ronald May, Sr. Marie Therese Fenton, RSM, and Susan and José Feliciano for their helpful ideas and useful suggestions.

To the staff and colleagues at Hartford Seminary, for providing me with the opportunity to assemble my thoughts and materials on the topic that eventually led to this book.

To Dr. Miriam Therese Winter, MMS, teacher and friend, who was a special mentor during my years at Hartford Seminary. Many of my reflections were sparked from observing her compassionate sensitivity to the poor, the sick, and the aged. I will remain ever grateful to her.

To Gwen Costello, publisher of Twenty-Third Publications, and the editorial staff for their invaluable assistance and support. May God bless them in abundance!

Contents

—Introduction—

Sick or elderly persons who are confined to healthcare facilities, hospitals, or at home, whether for a short or long term, often sense a feeling of isolation and loneliness. Some suffer a loss of independence and often experience deep insecurity, especially if they are unable to get around without the use of a walker or wheelchair. It becomes a harsh reality for those who at one time were able to enjoy engaging in outdoor activities, driving, or traveling, to face the truth that now they are not able to get around to do even the smallest task without the assistance of another person. The ability to go to the parish church to attend Mass or to enjoy camaraderie with other parishioners at various church functions becomes impossible due to their lack of strength and stamina. And most difficult for many of the sick and aged is the reality that they are no longer in contact with people outside their home with whom they could interact and from whom they could learn what is happening in their church and community. The world becomes quite small for them.

Yet there are creative ways for caring people to expand the world of the sick and the elderly. By sharing time with them, extending a compassionate hand, a prayerful heart, loving eyes, and sensitive ears, other people can bring to those confined at home the face of the healing Christ and help to make a significant difference in their lives.

Personal experiences with illness and long-time associations with elderly people, have brought me a special appreciation for those who face these "shut-in" conditions. I have gained much inspiration from their acceptance, a greater understanding of their endurance, and a keener awareness of some of their needs. Moreover, the several years of involvement in caring for my own mother, until her death at age 97, have enabled me to know how important spiritual, emotional, and physical support is for them. I have also come to realize that regardless of gender, race, geographical location, social or economic status, in sickness or old age there are needs that remain basic and similar to everyone.

This book identifies ways in which parishes can give evidence of being a healing community for their sick and elderly members. Beginning with a presentation of scriptural views on suffering and healing, I show how the healing mission of Christ is extended through a network of volunteers who engage in sacramental, spiritual, and charitable acts of service. Through a special ministry of care, a parish is able to respond to the needs of its shut-in parishioners, and thus make the healing power of Christ visible to them. The goal of a parish's ministry of care is to see that the Homebound are Encouraged through Assistance in Love. This assistance is provided by prayer, presence, and performances in a ministry outreach named Project H.E.A.L. The diverse forms of service flowing from this outreach are described in detail. I have provided suggestions that include participation by children and adults, and that are a result of firsthand involvement during my ministry to the sick and elderly in various parishes. It is my hope that this book will assist pastoral leaders in their endeavors to explore new ways to expand their ministry with increased fervor and commitment. I also hope that what is written will serve as an incentive and practical guide for those who seek to begin a ministry of care for ailing and aging parishioners in their faith community.

CHAPTER ONE

Suffering & Healing in Scripture

In the Hebrew Scriptures, sickness is generally portrayed as punishment for disobedience or sin. If the commandments were broken, the consequence was often the wrath of Yahweh accompanied by suffering and immeasurable pain. Healing in Jewish thought was associated with forgiveness or a reward. The following passages are examples of these views:

O Lord, do not rebuke me in your anger, or discipline me in your wrath.
For your arrows have sunk into me, and your hand has come down on me.
There is no soundness in my flesh because of your indignation; there is no health in my bones because of my sin.
For my iniquities have gone over my head; they weigh like a burden too heavy for me

Psalm 38:1–4

But if you will not obey me, and do not observe all these commandments, if you spurn my statutes, and abhor my ordinances, so that you will not observe all my commandments, and you break my covenant, I in turn will do this to you: I will bring terror on you; consumption and fever that waste the eyes and cause life to pine away. You shall sow your seed in vain, for your enemies shall eat it. *Leviticus 26:14–16*

"If you will listen carefully to the voice of the Lord your God, and do what is right in his sight, and give heed to his commandments and keep all his statutes, I will not bring upon you any of the diseases that I brought upon the Egyptians; for I am the Lord who heals you." *Exodus 15:26*

A clear picture of the notion that wounds endured on behalf of the guilty bring about healing is seen in the image of the Suffering Servant found in the Book of Isaiah:

> Surely he has borne our infirmities and carried our diseases; yet we accounted him stricken, struck down by God, and afflicted. But he was wounded for our transgressions, crushed for our iniquities; upon him was the punishment that made us whole, and by his bruises we are healed. *Isaiah 53:4–5*

Healing is a power which brings wholeness to what is broken, union to what is separated, strength to what is weak. New Testament accounts depict healing as a central ministry of the early Christian community. The miracles of Jesus and the apostles portray sickness and disease in connection with the search for healing. Throughout his entire life, Jesus visibly used his healing power to bring wholeness, strength, peace, and recovery to people in their illnesses, wounded relationships, and hurts of body, mind, and soul. These excerpts from the evangelists give us a glimpse of this mission.

> That evening they brought to him many who were possessed with demons; and he cast out the spirits with a word, and cured all who were sick. This was to fulfill what had been spoken through the prophet Isaiah, "He took our infirmities and bore our diseases." *Matthew 8:16–17*

> They brought to him a deaf man who had an impediment in his speech; and they begged him to lay his hand on him. He took him aside in private, away from the crowd, and put his fingers into his ears, and he spat and touched his tongue. Then looking up to heaven, he sighed and said to him, "Ephphatha," that is, "Be opened." And immediately his ears were opened, his tongue was released, and he spoke plainly. *Mark 7:32–37*

> John summoned two of his disciples and sent them to the Lord to ask, "Are you the one who is to come, or are we to wait for another?" And Jesus answered them, "Go and tell John what you have seen and heard: the blind receive their sight, the lame walk, the lepers are cleansed, the deaf hear, the dead are raised, the poor have good news brought to them." *Luke 7:18–22*

When Jesus healed, he employed various means. Sometimes he healed in response to a person's plea or to requests made by relatives or friends. At other times, Jesus healed without being asked but simply to demonstrate the love of God, as in the case of the man born blind. He restored people to health by a touch, a word, or a mixture of spittle or clay. And the gospels record that Jesus never refused anyone seeking healing. He merely looked into their heart, saw their faith, and answered their requests.

Old Testament theology taught that suffering and pain came from God. In the New Testament, however, Jesus changed this notion, telling people that suffering does not come from God; healing does. Jesus went about his ministry on earth preaching and healing. His methods of healing were signs of love and salvation, culminated in his saving death on the cross.

The apostles extended this healing ministry of Jesus after his ascension. They followed his example by preaching the Good News and healing those who approached them. The words of

Peter to the crippled beggar at the gate of the temple clearly relate to their mission: "I have no silver or gold, but what I have I give you; in the name of Jesus Christ of Nazareth, stand up and walk" (Acts 3:1–7).

The Church's caring concern for the sick and the elderly stems from Jesus' mandate to his apostles when he called them together and empowered them to carry on his role as healer:

> Then Jesus called the twelve together and gave them power and authority over all
> demons and to cure diseases, and he sent them out to proclaim the kingdom of God
> and to heal. *Luke 9:1–2*

In the gospels, Jesus often connected the healing of bodies with the healing of souls through the forgiveness of sin. In Luke 5:20, Jesus said to the paralytic, "Your sins are forgiven you," then he proceeded to restore him to health.

The healing ministry of Jesus and the apostles continues today through the Church. Just as Jesus healed people's spirits by forgiveness of sin and by reconciling them to God's love, so do the ordained priests of the Church bring healing through the sacraments.

Christ's healing gifts of peace and forgiveness are offered today particularly in the sacrament of reconciliation. Moreover, celebration of this sacrament not only gives us the opportunity to be reconciled with God, but also with one another. We are members of the Mystical Body of Christ, and whatever good we choose to do or to omit affects the entire Body of Christ. The sacrament of penance provides opportunities for us to confess our sins, to acknowledge our repentance, and to accept the absolution by the priest for forgiveness and restored healing and peace.

Closely related to the sacrament of reconciliation is the sacrament of the anointing of the sick. The evangelists relate that the Twelve carried out their commission by laying hands on the sick and they "anointed with oil many who were sick and cured them" (Mark 6:13).

St. James gave explicit exhortations on the reception of this sacrament in his letter.

> Are any among you sick? They should call for the elders of the church and have them
> pray over them, anointing them with oil in the name of the Lord. The prayer of faith
> will save the sick, and the Lord will raise them up; and anyone who has committed sins
> will be forgiven. *James 5:13–15*

Through the sacrament of the anointing of the sick, the Church continues to reach out to the sick and the elderly, expressing the same Christ-like concern and prayer for healing that were characteristic of the early Christian community. In the sacred anointing with blessed oil upon the forehead and hands, prayerful intercession is made for one who is seriously ill, physically, emotionally, or psychologically, or for one who is experiencing the weakness of old age. The sick and the elderly who receive this sacrament with faith and prayerful surrender, often experience healing strength and sometimes complete healing of the body.

In the sacrament of the Eucharist, Jesus gives us himself. Although we may be broken in body, we live in his divine life and share in his glorious resurrection. This sacrament brings his healing power to broken members of his Body. We read of Christ's participation in our brokenness in this passage from John's gospel:

Jesus said to them, "My Father who gives you the true bread from heaven. For the bread of God is that which comes down from heaven and gives life to the world." They said to him, "Sir, give us this bread always." Jesus said to them, "I am the bread of life. Whoever comes to me will never be hungry, and whoever believes in me will never be thirsty." *John 6:32–35*

The Holy Eucharist strengthens our relationships within the human family. In this sacrament of unity, we are united as brothers and sisters in Christ. We seek healing so that we might become healers for others. We become mindful of our responsibility to share Christ's life with brothers and sisters who long to feel the healing touch of solicitude and charity.

Scripture relates numerous examples of Christ's compassionate response to the sufferings of body and soul without regard for people's age or condition. The sacramental life of the Church is an accessible channel through which Christ's loving presence and healing power continue to be manifested to us at various ages and stages of life and in whatever pain we face spiritually, mentally, or physically. Each sacrament is a sign of the healing love of Christ, gifting us with grace for our life's journey.

Scriptural prayers for healing are cited in chapter four where specific forms of spiritual assistance are given for offering prayerful support to shut-ins.

The Catholic Church celebrates seven sacraments. However, I have chosen to focus attention on the three sacraments that apply to ministry with the sick and the elderly: reconciliation for "inner healing"; the anointing of the sick for "physical healing"; and the Holy Eucharist for "healing nourishment."

A description of the specific role of the sacraments in the ministry to the sick and the elderly through Project H.E.A.L. will be given at greater length in chapter three, where I will also give concrete examples of the efficacy of sacramental prayer through the personal testimonies that were shared with me.

CHAPTER TWO

Ministering through Project H.E.A.L.

Committed people enable and evoke commitment from others by the ways in which they themselves "walk" with others through the crises of their lives, giving them courage to draw new meaning and purpose from their burdens and trials.

Regis Duffy, *A Roman Catholic Theology of Pastoral Care*

These words of Regis Duffy appropriately sum up the reasons why a parish outreach such as Project H.E.A.L is important. His quote reminds us of the attitude that everyone should have in caring for the homebound. Although we may be unable to take away the physical ailments of our sick and elderly, we should make every effort to bring Christ's presence into their suffering, walk with them, and help them transform their conditions with purposeful living. And we should manifest this caring face through our assistance in love.

In our sophisticated computer age, despite all the modern technological advances of society and all the scientific resources of medicine, many sick and elderly persons continue to experience terrible suffering of mind and body. Some are isolated from society and must cope with these adverse realities alone. Some are distressed by the lack of concern and insensitivity they find in others, even in their own family or relatives. Some have few or no surviving family members, and yearn for the kindness and thoughtfulness of someone who will offer them the touch of compassion to uplift their spirits. And there are those who, despite their individual persistent prayer for strength and courage to go on, ask where they might turn for help in order to live more peacefully, knowing that they will never recover from their debilitating condition.

Jesus, our divine healer, took on the experience of suffering humanity. He spent most of his public life in the ministry of healing, teaching his followers by example to do the same, to heal one another, to open our hearts in gentle compassion to those in pain, and to help mend the brokenness of others. Yet there are still sick and elderly people who feel abandoned, who yearn for companionship, and who seek to be connected with caring people to help them in their needs.

One reliable source of help for the sick, the elderly, and the disabled, should be the parish. Since membership in most churches already includes persons who are sick or old, it should automatically imply that some form of ministry exists for them. Too often however, although shut-ins may receive the Holy Eucharist from a priest or lay minister monthly or weekly, the reception of this sacrament is the only form of service they receive from their parish. Because priests and lay ministers may have to bring Communion to several parishioners on the same day, their visits with individual shut-ins are often shortened and leave no opportunities for sharing longer conversations or for providing for spiritual and physical needs. Moreover, if the parish does not update the sick list regularly, names of sick or elderly parishioners may be omitted. This exclusion may cause persons who desire to receive the Eucharist in their homes to be overlooked. It could also deprive them of the possibility of receiving other attention from people in the parish or in the community.

In addition to the reception of the Holy Eucharist, parishes should extend their ministry by providing opportunities that offer their homebound parishioners other services to support them in their psychological, spiritual, or physical needs. At times, the assumption seems to be that it is not necessary to offer other forms of service to sick and elderly parishioners because relatives and friends supply their needs. This attitude, however, shows a certain weakness in response to God's call to assist the sick, disabled and elderly. Yet, there are people who would be willing to reach out to help the homebound but do not, either because they do not know how or because they are not given the freedom to do so.

Indeed, there are ailing and aging parishioners who need ongoing spiritual, emotional, and charitable support. They need to experience the benefit of spending time with someone who will offer a comforting presence, assuring words, shared prayer, inspirational reading and performance of errands. In addition to the reception of the Eucharist, shut-ins need opportunities for regularly celebrating the sacraments of reconciliation and anointing of the sick. They also need physical and emotional support through visitations that will enable them to interact with faith-filled people.

A parish responsibility

Yet how can they come to enjoy more moments for sharing love and for being loved, for speaking and for listening, for giving and for receiving? How can the healing mission of Jesus visibly be extended to them in such a manner? In essence, it is the responsibility of every parish to fulfill the gospel mandate to bring the healing presence of Jesus to those in need. In loving compassion, the parish is called to reach out to their sick and elderly parishioners and to be for them a special healing community. Project H.E.A.L. where Homebound are Encouraged through Assistance in Love, is one way in which a pastoral response to this call can be made.

Implementation of this outreach can begin with a survey taken in the parish by the priests and lay volunteers to determine who the ailing and aging parishioners are and where they are located: at home, in healthcare facilities, or in hospitals. Information for the survey can be obtained through telephone calls or letters to parishioners listed in the parish census file, especially to those whose households already include sick, elderly, or disabled members. Requests for information may also be obtained through announcements at the Sunday liturgies and through the weekly church bulletins. Families are encouraged to contact the parish office as soon as possible to provide information on their sick and elderly members. Students in religious education classes are also invited to seek out names of sick and elderly people in their homes and neighborhoods who could benefit from the parish ministry of care.

Recruitment for volunteers to serve in Project H.E.A.L. is made first, by a review of names of parishioners recommended by parish leaders; second, through personal invitation; and third, solicited through parish announcements and notices in the parish bulletins.

The successful outcome of the volunteer recruitment and of the positive response in obtaining current information on sick, disabled, or elderly parishioners, will depend upon the initiative and enthusiasm of parish leaders. How the sick and elderly become the focus of a parish's genuine concern, and how a parish begins to recognize the shut-ins' unique gifts to the community, will determine whether or not a parish is ready to launch an expanded ministry of care.

An important point to emphasize to parishioners who show an interest in becoming volunteers is that they pray and reflect seriously on God's call to them in this ministry. Before making any commitment to serve their sick and aging brothers and sisters in the parish, they need to ponder prayerfully on the particular ways they will share their time, energy, and individual gifts without interrupting family responsibilities. Hence, they need to consider carefully the importance of their role in ministry to shut-ins and of the immense impact they make upon them. Service in this parish outreach brings a two-fold blessing: to the volunteers who give the service and to the ailing parishioners who receive it. Moreover, the personal interaction between the person who is ministering and the person being ministered to is an experience that not only brings mutual inspiration, but also an empowerment for both to receive special graces.

There are three areas of involvement in Project H.E.A.L. in which parishioners are invited to serve. These consist of sacramental, spiritual, and charitable forms of service. When volunteers are recruited, they are given options on how they prefer to share their prayer, presence, and performances in any or all of these three areas. Children are also encouraged to participate in these dimensions of service by assisting the adult volunteers through their creative skills and musical talents. All members of the Project H.E.A.L. team—children and adults—become involved in ways that reflect their personal charisms and in the areas most conducive to their home and work schedules. Some may commit themselves to leadership roles by acting as coordinators of particular aspects of ministry. Others may choose to engage in specific projects from their homes. But in whatever way members share their time and talent, they soon become aware of the truth that when they choose to love by giving, they are receiving at the same time.

A sample letter, used to introduce parishioners to Project H.E.A.L. and to invite them to become participants, is included in chapter 8. In addition to a description of the various areas of involvement, this letter includes a tear-off section on which a person may respond with choices for rendering service and with written comments or suggestions.

The chart in chapter eight includes specific kinds of involvement rendered under the three headings of service which can be offered in a parish ministry of care. It is hoped that this chart will serve as a guide for implementing more activities on behalf of parish shut-ins or for inciting new ideas to add in the respective columns listed under the sacramental, spiritual, and charitable headings.

CHAPTER THREE

Healing through the Sacraments

The sacramental phase of Project H.E.A.L. focuses on providing opportunities for the sick and the elderly parishioners to celebrate the sacraments of holy Eucharist, reconciliation, and anointing of the sick. Those who desire to receive these sacraments are asked to make known their requests either by notifying the parish priests themselves or through someone else who could make the contact for them, such as a parish visitor, a relative, or a caregiver.

The celebration of the Eucharist is the central act of our Catholic Christian life and the highest form of worship. When we receive the Body and Blood of Christ in the Eucharist, we partake of the Real Presence in a special way, and are not only in intimacy with Jesus, but also in solidarity with others. We are bonded with Christ and with brothers and sisters in the family of the Church and the world. The Eucharist nourishes our bodies as well as our souls and brings us to a healing experience as we commune with the divine Healer. Each time we are at Mass, we are literally at a healing service. Before receiving Communion, we pray: "Lord, I am not worthy to receive you, but only say the word and I shall be healed." In receiving this sacrament, the sick and the elderly are given the opportunity to invite the risen Lord to transform their condition into opportunities for redemptive suffering. They are nourished with newfound strength and hope.

If the sick and the elderly are unable to attend the liturgical celebrations of Eucharist in their parish church, Holy Communion is brought to them at their residence by a priest, deacon, or lay minister of the Eucharist. Many parishes conduct liturgies in the nursing homes, enabling shut-ins to receive the Eucharist and also the Anointing during those services.

In the sacrament of reconciliation, the sick and elderly are given the chance to be reconciled with God and others. They are reminded of the spiritual benefits connected to this sacrament and are encouraged to receive it for greater peace and inner healing. In accepting the opportunity for confession, the priest's absolution, and the special grace of this sacrament, recipients often gain new strength to accept their suffering with purpose, new fervor to unite their cross with the Cross of Christ, and a new resolve to pray for others, for the Church, and for the world. Although this sacrament is not always welcomed with the same anticipation as other sacraments, shut-ins are encouraged to focus on the loving forgiveness of God and the Church and on being assured of God's unconditional love for them. Moreover, in celebrating reconciliation or penance, they are disposed to receive the sacraments of the Eucharist and the anointing of the sick with greater joy.

The sacrament of the anointing of the sick is specifically for persons who seek prayer for healing in times of serious illness. When Jesus and the apostles demonstrated their compassionate regard for the sick, they blessed and anointed them for healing and commissioned their successors to do the same. However, by the ninth century, after a period of questionable practices and abuses, the anointing took on an entirely different meaning, and was given a new name. The sacrament became known as Extreme Unction. The Church viewed this sacrament as the last anointing or the death-bed sacrament, reserved only for those who faced the critical or final stage of life.

In 1962, directives from the Second Vatican Council called for a revision of many Church practices, and among them was the return to the original concept of this sacrament. The anointing of the sick for healing of the whole person replaced the old notion of Extreme Unction. Any baptized Catholic who has the use of reason, and is in the state of grace, is encouraged to receive this anointing when suffering from a serious illness, physically, mentally or psychologically. The elderly who experience weakness from their age, although not facing any serious illness, are also encouraged to receive this sacrament and reminded not to put off the anointing. Many elderly people still maintain the old notion that one must be dying in order to be anointed and fail to realize that by virtue of their age, they should accept the sacramental anointing for healing strength.

During the Middle Ages, it was the custom to anoint the eyes, ears, nostrils, mouth, hands and feet, and to pray for forgiveness for any sin committed through the use of them. The use of oil in the anointing can be traced back to biblical times when it was a symbolic gesture for making something sacred or for bringing the Spirit of Yahweh upon a person.

The current rite of anointing for the sick involves the silent laying on of hands by the priest over the person, and the anointing with blessed oil, tracing a cross first on the forehead and next on the palm of each hand while saying the following prayers:

Through this holy anointing, may the Lord in his love and mercy, help you with the grace of the Holy Spirit.
The recipient responds: Amen.

May the Lord who frees you from sin save you and raise you up.
The recipient responds: Amen.

Bishops' Committee on the Liturgy, Study Text 2, *Pastoral Care of the Sick and Dying*

Although the revised rite of the sacramental anointing focuses on God's healing power rather than on preparation for death, those who are critically ill or dying may receive the last rites. The priest prays, administers a "last" anointing, and gives them a "last" Eucharist or Holy Viaticum, to help them in their final stage of life.

The healing power of prayer

The sacrament of the sick today regards the anointing rite as a celebration experience which may take place privately at home, in healthcare facilities, in hospitals, or in a largely attended parish setting. Family members, relatives, and friends are encouraged to celebrate the sacramental anointing with the sick or elderly person and to participate in the prayers on their behalf. Thus the sacrament becomes a faith-filled experience that is welcomed joyfully and gratefully for the healing presence of Christ.

When we are in terrible pain and face unresolved medical problems, it becomes easy to doubt God's loving care for us. The sacrament of the anointing empowers us with the strength to accept and surrender our heavy burdens and sometimes also brings healing of the body, such as remission of a physical malady, cure of an addiction, or recovery from an illness. The following attest to the efficacy of prayer in this sacrament:

Susan was a nurse who participated with the medical personnel at a parish celebration of the anointing of the sick where I served in ministry. She told me that as she celebrated the anointing and Eucharist during that Mass, she prayed for healing from the severe alcohol problem that had plagued her for many years. When I met her recently, she happily informed me that she was free of her addiction and gratefully enjoys the sobriety which began at the anointing several years ago.

When Maria was a teenager, she was given little hope for surviving lymphatic cancer. Two of her relatives had died of the same form of cancer. Bone-marrow transplants turned out to be problematic, and doctors painted a grim picture of her future. She was warned of the great risks she would encounter if she married and bore children. But Maria refused to let the doctors' prognosis dampen her positive disposition, and she was determined not to let her physical condition impede her life's ambitions. She decided to put all her energy into praying for healing through the sacraments. I recall the many times she would contact me to join her in prayer and would ask me to arrange for the parish priest to celebrate Mass in her home when she was too weak to attend Church services. She frequently asked to celebrate the sacraments of the Eucharist and anointing of the sick, and encouraged her sick and elderly family members to do the same. Today, Maria's cancer is in full remission, and she is happily married with three healthy children. She attributes her miraculous healing to prayer, especially in the sacraments of the Eucharist and the anointing of the sick.

Kevin was ten years of age and suffered from an inoperable brain tumor. I visited him often, bringing the Holy Eucharist and sharing prayer for him with his two younger sisters and parents. Although his mother was a non-Catholic, she respected the faith of her husband and children and would participate silently in the prayers for Kevin. She often joined her family when they celebrated the Sunday liturgies in the parish church and also accompanied them when they prepared for the reception of reconciliation or attended other church functions. She sat next to Kevin during the parish anointing of the sick, reverently observing every movement in the liturgical celebration.

The day Kevin's condition worsened, I received a phone call from his mother, asking me to rush to their home. She was unsuccessful in reaching the parish priest but, realizing how Kevin loved to receive the Eucharist, asked if I would bring him the sacrament. When I arrived at their home, Kevin's parents and sisters were kneeling at his bedside. He had expired at the same time I was parking my car across their street. We hugged, cried, and prayed together. The Eucharist which was intended for Kevin, was later given to his sisters and followed by prayer that God grant eternal rest to Kevin and healing strength to one another. As we waited for the doctor and funeral director to arrive at the home, we stood prayerfully encircled around Kevin. We offered blessing prayers upon him and praised God for releasing him from the suffering he long endured. We also prayed with gratitude that Kevin had finally come to enjoy the fullness of God's healing power in heaven.

A year after Kevin's death, his mother informed me that she wanted to become a Catholic. She was of the Jewish faith but found healing inspiration in her son's love for the Catholic beliefs. She was particularly edified by his reverence and appreciation for the sacraments, especially the Eucharist, and she desired to partake of this sacrament, too. She enrolled in the Rite of Christian Initiation (RCIA) at the parish and prepared to enter her new faith life which was inspired by Kevin when he prepared to enter into his new life with God. The healing effects of the sacraments were indeed visible in Kevin's family.

My own elderly mother, who died two months short of her ninety-seventh birthday, would regain strength and peace whenever a priest celebrated with her the sacraments of Eucharist, reconciliation, and anointing of the sick. There was always a noticeable difference in her ability to move about and a tranquility in her countenance after she received these sacraments.

Spiritual healing has widespread effects

During a meeting with parishioners to plan for a communal celebration of the anointing, I was approached by a woman who asked if it would be possible for me to visit her husband, Richard, at their home. He had recently undergone open heart surgery and was not recovering as well as they expected. She hoped that he would be receptive to receiving this sacrament, if not in church, sometime in the near future at home. I assured her that I would visit and bring him some religious pamphlets to pave the way for the priest. When I arrived at their home, Richard was cordial and received me warmly. Our chat centered around prayer for healing and the spiritual benefits gained when receiving the sacraments. He admitted that he had not been to confession in years, voicing his apprehension and admitting his deep fears about seeing a priest. He became quiet and pensive and after a brief hesitation, began to express sadness and concern about the gravity of his condition. He admitted his need for the sacraments and agreed to see a priest. Soon after my visit with him, Richard contacted the pastor of the parish and asked to receive the sacraments of reconciliation and Eucharist. Father saw him the following day and recommended that he receive the sacrament of the anointing of the sick during his next home visit. Richard consented to Father's offer and also asked if he could invite others to receive this sacrament with him. He thought that perhaps his ailing brother and elderly aunt would like to attend the home gathering and celebrate the anointing, too.

I accompanied our pastor to Richard's home the following week for a celebration of the sacrament of the sick. To our amazement, the house was filled with relatives and friends who had come to join Richard, his brother, and aunt to support them in prayer on this "joy-filled" occasion. The active participation in that home liturgy was a moving spiritual experience and became the topic of many conversations that followed. My recollections of that evening continue to bring me healing inspiration.

Richard died peacefully a few months later; his brother's health gradually improved; and his aunt's difficult aging process was accepted more gracefully. The healing power of Christ was indeed in each of them through the sacraments and through everyone who supported them with their love and prayer.

I myself was blessed with healing after a priest gave me the Anointing of the Sick in the emergency room of a Pennsylvania hospital while I suffered from an unusually high fever. I distinctly recall the healing effects of this sacramental prayer offered for me at that time.

These healing accounts are only a few of the many which I have witnessed over the course of years in ministry. Yet the same elements of truth and faith were found in every one of the healing experiences; namely, that God's saving grace in the sacraments and God's healing power in the recipients were clearly manifested and had lasting effects.

The parish celebration of the sacrament of the anointing of the sick usually takes place during a Eucharistic Liturgy. Some parishes hold the celebration in conjunction with National Shut-In Day, the third Sunday of October, or during Pastoral Care Week, commemorated in hospitals during the fourth week of October. Other parishes plan the sacramental anointing during periods of warm weather in order to facilitate the transporting of people from their places of residence to the church. The anointing may also take place in a healthcare facility every few months during a Mass or prayer service. In addition to those who will be anointed at this liturgy for the sick, participation involves the community of priests, parishioners, family members, friends, medical personnel, and members of Project H.E.A.L. All gather together in prayerful solidarity for their sick and elderly brothers and sisters.

Members of the medical profession are invited to participate as readers or eucharistic ministers and assist the sick and elderly to position their hands during the anointing rite. They also join everyone in the parish hall for fellowship and refreshments. Their presence is both spiritually and psychologically uplifting. Since many recipients are patients of these doctors and nurses who ordinarily care for their physical needs in the hospital or health facilities, they become inspired at seeing them participate in this spiritual experience with prayerful support for them. They are uplifted to see these medical persons seek the blessings of the divine Physician on their behalf. At the same time, the presence of doctors and nurses in the congregation provides a "safe" feeling for the sick and elderly, bringing them psychological reassurance. They know that they will be given attention if medical assistance is needed during the liturgy.

The parish celebration of the Liturgy of Anointing becomes a special source of involvement for children as well as adult members in the Ministry of Care. The ailing parishioners are helped as they enter and leave the church; are given transportation if they need it, and served refreshments following the liturgy. The youth offer assistance by decorating and setting up the tables in the parish hall, serving the parishioners, and cleaning up after the coffee hour.

Indeed, there are diverse ways in which a parish can provide opportunities for their suffering members to enjoy the sacramental life of the church. What a blessing it is, not only for the recipients of the sacramental anointing but for the entire parish, to know that the sick and the elderly are made the main focus of a liturgical celebration! And parishes can continue to "be there" for their sick and elderly members through other ways of prayerful support. Besides the reception of the sacraments, shut-ins can enjoy being spiritually uplifted through religious literature, inspirational music, and prayer partners. These forms of spiritual service will be discussed in the next chapter.

Chapter Four

Extending Prayerful Support

There are various ways in which ministers of care can extend their prayerful presence with the sick and elderly. Some times it is rendered through a telephone prayer line or by special remembrances in private or communal prayer. At other times, it is extended through formal or informal prayer, scripture sharing, recitation of the rosary, or quiet reflection on the messages of prayer cards shared at the times of their visits. Religious books, magazines, or pamphlets for spiritual reading, and inspirational videos and cassettes, can equally provide prayerful support to them. Another means is through the invitation to the parish community to remember them prayerfully in the Book of Intentions and the General Intercessions at Mass. Children in the parish school or Religious Education programs could include the names of the sick and elderly parishioners in their special prayers before class.

Spiritual support may also come through the media, particularly the Eternal Word Television Network (EWTN) and the Archdiocesan sponsored religious programs on radio and television, allowing the shut-ins to watch the Mass and to unite in solidarity with others who watch and pray through the TV liturgy. In Connecticut, for example, priests celebrate Mass daily on television to benefit those in hospitals and nursing homes as well as the homebound. Some Catholic hospitals present the Mass live through closed circuit TV for those who are non-ambulatory. Parish visitors bring missalettes to their shut-ins on a monthly basis, giving them the opportunity to follow the Mass and to reflect on the liturgical season and scripture readings of the day.

A children's music ministry can bring inspiration and entertainment to the sick and elderly by visiting them to share musical talents. A special dimension of healing flows from the singing of religious songs by children. Those who hear their voices and see their joy-filled smiles are always comforted and uplifted in spirit.

The kinds of prayerful gestures mentioned here are certainly not all-inclusive. However, they do give a clear picture of the diverse forms of service a parish may fulfill in rendering spiritual support to their shut-ins. These forms also bring powerful manifestations of God's healing love for the sick and the elderly. Although such services differ from the sacramental forms of service and do not replace the healing grace of the sacraments, they do nourish and enrich the faith life of the shut-ins and leave a special impact upon them spiritually. Moreover, regardless of where, when, or how the faith life of a volunteer is shared with a shut-in, the spiritual exchange between the giver and the receiver is special, uplifting, and inspirational to both.

To some leaders, the areas of spiritual service mentioned here may seem quite common and may already be taking place in their parishes. For others, information on certain kinds of spiritual service may either be totally unfamiliar to them or not sufficient for them in their attempts to expand their parish involvement. It is also possible that particular types of service which could benefit sick and elderly parishioners, are not offered because an opportunity for doing so is lacking.

In an attempt to address some of these issues and to offer help in starting new forms of parish involvement, attention will be directed to five specific areas of service which proved rewarding during my ministry to the sick and elderly. It is hoped that in describing these areas, a spark of enthusiasm will ignite for trying something new on behalf of ailing parishioners. The five areas are:

- scriptural prayer

- telephone hotline

- prayer cards

- Children's Music Ministry: Spirit Joy

- spiritual adoption.

Scriptural Prayer

In addition to their formal and informal kinds of prayer with shut-ins, Project H.E.A.L. members found that prayerfully reflecting on selected Scripture passages was a key aspect of spiritual support in their visitations to the homebound. After reading and pondering on various Bible passages, they selected those that were particularly meaningful in their spiritual sharing and recorded them on paper. These passages were then shared with other members and compiled without duplication. The final compilation became a helpful guide to all the members for use in their praying for healing. The scriptural references were taken from the Old and New Testaments and include thirty-three passages that relate to the healing power of God. These passages are:

Turn, O Lord, save my life; deliver me for the sake of your steadfast love.
The Lord has heard my supplication; the Lord accepts my prayer. *Psalm 6:4, 9*

O Lord my God, I cried to you for help, and you have healed me. *Psalm 30:2*

The Lord sustains them on their sickbed; in their illness you heal all their infirmities.
As for me, I said, "O Lord, be gracious to me; heal me, for I have sinned against you."
Psalm 41:3–4

Why are you cast down, O my soul, and why are you disquieted within me? Hope in God; for I shall again praise him, my help and my God. *Psalm 42:11*

Because you have made the Lord your refuge, the Most High your dwelling place,
no evil shall befall you, no scourge come near your tent.
For he will command his angels concerning you to guard you in all your ways.
On their hands they will bear you up, so that you will not dash your foot against a stone. *Psalm 91:9–12*

Bless the Lord, O my soul, and do not forget all his benefits—
who forgives all your iniquity, who heals all your diseases. *Psalm 103:2–3*

Trust in the Lord with all your heart, and do not rely on your own insight.
In all your ways acknowledge him, and he will make straight your paths.
Do not be wise in your own eyes; fear the Lord, and turn away from evil.
It will be a healing for your flesh and a refreshment for your body. *Proverbs 3:5–8*

My child, be attentive to my words; incline your ear to my sayings.
Do not let them escape from your sight; keep them within your heart.
For they are life to those who find them, and healing to all their flesh. *Proverbs 4:20–22*

My child, when you are ill, do not delay, but pray to the Lord, and he will heal you.
Sirach 38:9

Surely he has borne our infirmities and carried our diseases; yet we accounted him stricken, struck down by God, and afflicted. But he was wounded for our transgressions, crushed for our iniquities; upon him was the punishment that made us whole, and by his bruises we are healed. *Isaiah 53:4–5*

Heal me, O Lord, and I shall be healed; save me, and I shall be saved; for you are my praise. *Jeremiah 17:14*

But for you who revere my name the sun of righteousness shall rise, with healing in its wings. *Malachi 4:2*

Jesus went throughout Galilee, teaching in their synagogues and proclaiming the good news of the kingdom and curing every disease and every sickness among the people.
Matthew 4:23

Jesus said, "Ask, and it will be given you; search, and you will find; knock, and the door will be opened for you. For everyone who asks receives, and everyone who searches finds, and for everyone who knocks, the door will be opened....If you who are evil, know how to give good gifts to your children, how much more will your Father in heaven give good things to those who ask him!" *Matthew 7:7–11*

And he said to him, "I will come and cure him."... And to the centurion Jesus said, "Go; let it be done for you according to your faith." And the servant was healed in that hour.
Matthew 8:7, 13, 17

Jesus said to them, "Do you believe that I am able to do this?" They said to him, "Yes, Lord." Then he touched their eyes and said, "According to your faith let it be done to you." And their eyes were opened. *Matthew 9:28–30*

When he went ashore, he saw a great crowd; and he had compassion for them and cured their sick. *Matthew 14:14*

Great crowds came to him, bringing with them the lame, the maimed, the blind, the mute, and many others. They put them at his feet, and he cured them. *Matthew 15:30*

"For truly I tell you, if you have faith the size of a mustard seed, you will say to this mountain, 'Move from here to there,' and it will move; and nothing will be impossible for you." *Matthew 17:20–21*

Large crowds followed him, and he cured them there. *Matthew 19:2*

And he cured many who were sick with various diseases, and cast out many demons.
Mark 1:34

Jesus said to her, "Daughter, your faith has made you well; go in peace, and be healed of your disease." *Mark 5:34*

Jesus said to him, "If you are able!—All things can be done for the one who believes."
Mark 9:23

Jesus said to him, "Go; your faith has made you well." Immediately he regained his sight and followed him on the way. *Mark 10:52*

Jesus answered them, "Have faith in God. Truly I tell you, if you say to this mountain, 'Be taken up and thrown into the sea,' and if you do not doubt in your heart, but believe that what you say will come to pass, it will be done for you. So I tell you, whatever you ask for in prayer, believe that you have received it, and it will be yours." *Mark 11:22–25*

And all in the crowd were trying to touch him, for power came out from him and healed all of them. *Luke 6:19*

Now in Jerusalem by the Sheep Gate there is a pool, called in Hebrew Beth-zatha, which has five porticoes. In these lay many invalids —blind, lame, and paralyzed. One man was there who had been ill for thirty-eight years. When Jesus saw him lying there and knew that he had been there a long time, he said to him, "Do you want to be made well?" The sick man answered him, "Sir, I have no one to put me into the pool when the water is stirred up; and while I am making my way, someone else steps down ahead of me." Jesus said to him, "Stand up, take your mat and walk." At once the man was made well, and he took up his mat and began to walk. *John 5:2–9*

Jesus said [to the man born blind], "Do you believe in the Son of Man?" He answered, "And who is he, sir? Tell me, so that I may believe in him." Jesus said to him, "You have seen him, and the one speaking with you is he." He said, "Lord, I believe." And he worshiped him. *John 9:35*

John preached how God anointed Jesus of Nazareth with the Holy Spirit and with power; how he went about doing good and healing all who were oppressed by the devil, for God was with him. *Acts 10:38*

So we do not lose heart. Even though our outer nature is wasting away, our inner nature is being renewed day by day. For this slight momentary affliction is preparing us for an eternal weight of glory beyond all measure, because we look not at what can be seen but at what cannot be seen; for what can be seen is temporary, but what cannot be seen is eternal. *2 Corinthians 4:16–18*

Who will separate us from the love of Christ? Will hardship, or distress, or persecution, or famine, or nakedness, or peril, or sword? No, in all these things we are more than conquerors through him who loved us. For I am convinced that neither death, nor life, nor angels, nor rulers, nor things present, nor things to come, nor powers, nor height, nor depth, nor anything else in all creation, will be able to separate us from the love of God in Christ Jesus our Lord. *Romans 8:35–38*

Are any among you sick? They should call for the elders of the church and have them pray over them, anointing them with oil in the name of the Lord. The prayer of faith will save the sick, and the Lord will raise them up; and anyone who has committed sins will be forgiven. *James 5:13–15*

He himself bore our sins in his body on the cross, so that, free from sins, we might live for righteousness; by his wounds you have been healed. *1 Peter 2:24*

Telephone Hot Line

The telephone is a convenient and practical means for connecting with the sick and elderly not only for friendly conversation, but also for reassurance and prayerful sharing. In addition to this one-to-one medium of communication, the parish sets up a twenty-four hour telephone prayer hot line. A dedicated team of "pray-ers" engage in intercessory prayer in response to telephone callers who request prayer for themselves or others with special needs. Service in this prayer ministry is open to everyone. But those who agree to be part of this aspect of Project H.E.A.L. are directed to follow a certain procedure for passing on the prayer requests to the members on the team in an unbroken line of communication. Names and telephone numbers of two leaders of the parish telephone hot line are published in the church bulletin along with a brief description of this spiritual ministry. Parishioners are invited to call either of them.

When a leader receives a call for prayer, he or she notifies the other team leader and they both begin the telephone line by each contacting one or two other persons, depending upon the number of participants in this prayer-line ministry. The members who are contacted by the leaders, in turn, pass on the prayer requests to others who also pass on the same intention until all members on the prayer line have been reached. One person is designated to be the last to be called in the line of order to ensure that the entire group of praying persons does in fact receive the requests. There is no limit to the number of calls received on the prayer hot line each day. However, when callers' requests are passed on, they are done with reverence and in a line of continuous intercessory prayer. Members may choose to pray in any manner they wish, as long as they pray for the callers' intentions promptly and fervently. The example shown involves fifteen persons on the prayer line who pass on telephone requests obtained by the leaders.

Procedure for Passing on Prayer Requests

A caller contacts Leader A, who then contacts B—or vice versa—and both begin the prayer line. #15 is designated as the last to be called.

• Leader A calls members 1 and 2, 1 calls 3, and 2 calls 4; 3 calls 5 and 4 calls 6 and both 5 and 6 call 7

• Leader B calls 8 and 9; 8 calls 10 and 9 calls 11; 10 calls 12 and 11 calls 13 and 12 and 13 call 14. Both 7 and 14 call 15.

• When both 7 and 14 call 15, the last on the line, this insures that the prayer requests have been reached everyone on the telephone hot line.

The powerful effects of this ministry have been evidenced in the responses received when persons return calls to say that their prayers have been answered.

Prayer Cards

Some of the inspirational cards shared with shut-ins were in the form of prayer-poems taken from my original collection *Reflective Whisperings*. Written during my own stages of illness, these prayer-poems have been distributed to sick and elderly people in various places and have been a source of inspiration for persons facing difficult times in their physical or mental sufferings. The following poems are used on cards that continue to be circulated today among shut-ins at home, in hospitals, and in nursing homes. You can use these poems to make your own cards.

My Offering

Gracious and loving God,

These pains, old and new,

Are lovingly offered

As my gift to you.

Although so unpleasant

And heavy to bear,

They're filled with much meaning

When raised up in prayer.

For comfort and healing

I fervently pray,

But mostly for your strength

To bear them this day.

May each pain I suffer

Be offered to raise

This gift of myself now

With love and with praise.

God's Mosaic

I am in God's great mosaic

Pieced within creation's art;

Broken, shaped, and fitted neatly

As God's own selected part.

Without me, there would be missing

In this Master Plan above

That which God has chosen special

To complete his work of love.

Should I moan for being broken

And begin to question why,

I need only remember

God's mosaic from on high.

God's design portrays perfection

Fashioned, trimmed, and framed just right

Gently does God's love transform me

Through his hands of power and might.

Help me, God, and bless my efforts

To accept this shape of me;

Keep my place in your mosaic

Fixed in love eternally.

A Prayer for Trust

God, it's dark—I'm scared
grasp tightly my hand;
There's no sight ahead,
help me understand.

Show me the way to
deeper trust in You;
Anoint me with faith
to see love anew.

Let me believe that
through your healing touch
Hope's power will return
to strengthen me much.

Take hold of all fears,
the big ones and small;
With you at my side,
no need is too tall.

Teach me the truth that
Your grace fills all days;
These special moments
can give you more praise.

Thank you for listening
to my heartfelt prayer;
Thanks, too, for keeping
this child in your care.

I Believe

I believe that you are with me
in my climb up mountains tall;
And I know your Spirit guides me
as I cross paths big and small.

I believe that you are near me
tho' it seems you're out of sight;
Never do you leave my presence,
You are with me day and night.

I believe that you invite me
to take shelter in your Heart;
Without any force upon me
You await my willing start.

I believe that you assist me
in my times of pain and stress;
And you offer peaceful comfort
To restore true happiness.

I believe that you are gracious
as you follow my life's trend;
Trusting in your faithful promise,
I believe your love won't end.

Giving In

When life felt harsh and hope was lost,
in pity, I cried out:
Why is my God so far away?
Must I more loudly shout?
My efforts seem to be in vain;
tears flow into the night.
I'm strongly tempted to give up;
God seems nowhere in sight.

But then, I heard in whispered voice;
"Child, don't give up, give in.
Remember how on Calvary
Jesus died so you could win.
Surrender to my holy will;
accept this special call.
His "giving–in" fulfilled my plan;
He bore the cross for all."

I thought about God's gift of love,
the Paschal Mystery,
And gradually did recognize
the healing victory.
I prayed anew with greater trust,
repenting for all sin,
And felt a peaceful strength once more
the moment I gave in.

Recognize the Lord

Recognize me, little child
in every phase of life;
See me in your happy times
As well as those of strife.

Recognize my presence strong
when trials seem too much,
Feel my overwhelming strength;
accept my gentle touch.

Recognize my rays of hope
extending healing light;
I have not abandoned you
tho' fog obscures your sight.

Recognize my whispered voice
which speaks throughout your pains;
Listen to my message now;
its healing power sustains.

Recognize me in this scene,
think not I'm absent here;
Why would I leave as orphan
you whom I hold so dear?

Recognize me every day
in every single place;
Lift your eyes unto my own;
behold my love-filled face.

Children's Music Ministry: Spirit Joy

The idea of forming a children's music ministry came after prayerfully reflecting and sharing with a guitarist friend about the possibility of organizing a children's group to sing for the sick and elderly at our archdiocesan television Mass. Through the collaborative efforts of friends and musicians who were likewise interested in this endeavor, a brochure was prepared and circulated to introduce and explain the purpose of this ministry. The group was organized with children of relatives and friends as the first members. Later on, others who learned about the group joined them, bringing the membership to thirty-eight children ranging in age between seven and sixteen. Children qualified as members of Spirit Joy 1) if they were able to make the commitment to come to rehearsals twice a month to learn the songs and 2) if they were willing to travel to various places where sick and elderly people were the main audience.

This ministry came to be named Spirit Joy because of its goal: to bring the joy of the Holy Spirit to sick and elderly people through music. Members sang during the archdiocesan TV Mass each month, which is specifically for shut-ins. They also shared their music to benefit the sick and elderly in hospitals, nursing homes, and in parishes, especially during the communal celebrations of the anointing of the sick.

Eventually, with the help of Susan and José Feliciano, two compact discs of the group's songs, *Spirit Joy* Volume I and *Spirit Joy* Volume II. were produced. Each album includes sixteen original religious songs. This music has been a special gift to hospitals and healthcare facilities, as well as homes.

A children's music ministry in the parish not only allows the youth an opportunity to put to use their creative energies and musical talents, but, more importantly, enables them to reach out to ailing and elderly parishioners, bringing inspiration and joy through prayerful singing directed specifically to them.

Spiritual Adoption

Children and adults can spiritually adopt a person who is sick or old through daily prayerful remembrances of them. As a prayer-partner, the volunteer obtains the name of a parishioner who is homebound, in a hospital, or in a nursing home, and promises to remember that particular person in prayer each day. If possible, the volunteer may write to the prayer partner, telling of this spiritual adoption and personal pledge of prayer, and also send cards or notes of caring concern on special occasions.

The adoption of a shut-in for prayerful remembrances not only provides an opportunity for the sick and elderly to gain spiritual strength through the prayers offered for them, but also gives to those praying on their behalf a greater awareness of the sufferings that are endured and the redemptive implications associated with them.

CHAPTER FIVE

Sharing Head, Heart, & Hands in Love

The charitable dimension of ministry to the sick, disabled, and elderly involves donating time and talent and allows for more social interaction between the ailing person and the volunteer. By sharing head, heart and hands on their behalf, children and adults render assistance in a ministry of loving presence, compassionate listening, and charitable deeds as they strive to live out the corporal works of mercy.

Personal contact is made through friendly visitation and telephone reassurance. Yet, the art of listening with love and care is in itself a special ministry. In nursing homes, errands may include miscellaneous group activities as well as reading, writing letters, or story-telling to individuals. Volunteers are prepared to assist in any capacity necessary to meet the physical and emotional needs of those to whom they minister. Children also participate in this ministry by bringing pets, making crafts, writing cards, knitting lap blankets, playing games, entertaining with their music, making seasonal room decorations, and constructing special novelties for their food trays or tables.

The homebound may appreciate assistance such as shoveling snow, raking leaves, or shopping for them. Services may be rendered by one volunteer or by a group of volunteers who prefer to engage in a large project.

A brief description of some of the more popular charitable activities rendered by children and adult members follows.

Greeting Card Ministry

Various cards are either purchased, constructed with special computer designs and messages, or are hand-made with original art and script specifically for the shut-in. In matching envelopes, cards are made for individuals or for large groups and sent in celebration of the holy days, holidays, birthdays, or simply to express one's remembrance of the person. A large bulk of cards is sent to nursing homes or hospitals for distribution, particularly to those who have no family members or who rarely receive mail. This form of outreach is greatly welcomed by the shut-ins. Receiving cards that express care and thoughtful concern throughout the year helps them realize they are not forgotten.

Donating to the Parish Giving Tree

Parishioners are invited to place new or unused gifts under a designated tree in church during the weeks of Advent. An explanation of this parish project is given at the Mass prior to the first Sunday of Advent and also in the parish Sunday bulletins (see copy in chapter 8). The purpose of the Giving Tree is to donate items for distribution to the needy, the homebound, and those in nursing homes. A list of preferred items for the gift-giving is included with the explanation of this Advent project. Some of the requested donations include: towels, socks, pajamas, robes, night gowns, slippers, sweaters, tooth brushes, lotions, powder, linens, bed-shawls, jewelry, card or miscellaneous games, and note paper. More suggestions regarding the various kinds of gifts needed for shut-ins may also be obtained from staff members in the healthcare facilities.

Sticker-Sharing

Stickers come in all sorts of shapes and sizes with messages that include scripture sayings, religious captions, and cheery slogans. They are readily available for purchase from any religious supply company. Using stickers is a delightful way to help shut-ins in large groups interact with one another. When colorful stickers inscribed with large messages of hope, love and cheer are given to the sick and elderly in a group setting, they not only bring smiles and expressions of joy on the faces of the recipients, but also become focal points for happy conversations. They are particularly welcomed when distributed by children after their musical entertainment in nursing homes. Stickers often bring a wonderful ending to their sharing. Shut-ins appreciate receiving them and members enjoy sticking inspirational messages on their clothing.

Bringing Flowers and Plants

Deliveries of flowers and plants on occasions such as birthdays, Christmas, Valentine's Day, or Easter are indeed signs of thoughtfulness to the shut-ins and a source of much cheer to them. However, such deliveries do not have to be limited to special occasions. These gifts may be shared at other times of the year without any particular feast in mind. Local funeral homes often dispose of their excessive supply of flowers and would be glad to share them with the sick and elderly. Parishioners are encouraged to remember the shut-ins by donating flowers from their family events (after a jubilee, wedding, graduation, or anniversary celebration). The floral sections of local grocery stores often are willing to donate bundles of flowers or plants to nursing homes or individual shut-ins when parish ministers make this particular form of parish outreach known to them.

A special service project for students in the confirmation preparation program could include preparing bouquets for shut-ins, made from the large bundles of flowers donated by stores. Parish visitors may also bring the shut-ins some seeds, soil, and small pots or containers so that they themselves can plant a perennial or some other kind of greenery in their residence. By giving the necessary attention to their plant, regularly watering it and placing it in the sunlight, the shut-ins have the opportunity to watch the growth of their seedling and eventually see its transformation into a flower or plant.

Preparing Meals

Parishioners are invited to prepare meals for their ailing brothers and sisters who live in their own homes, alone or with another family member. If the sick or elderly are ambulatory or are able to move about in a wheel chair, they could be invited to enjoy a meal outside their homes with fellow parishioners. Preparing meals for shut-ins requires thoughtful planning, however, and the cooks must keep in mind that there are particular diets and foods which must be taken into consideration. In addition to sharing a delightful meal, this form of service is a wonderful way to share presence and camaraderie with those who live alone. Some healthcare facilities encourage volunteers to plan a menu and prepare special food to cook or bake with the residents. The opportunity to participate in this project would allow residents to enjoy the smell and touch of the food and enable them to recall pleasant memories of their own past experiences of cooking when they lived at home.

Providing Food Gifts

Sometimes during a visit, a member may detect a person's need for food. Food items are often made available from a parish's social action food bank, through baskets prepared by the parish's food drive or from generous parishioners who offer to prepare meals, bring baked goods, or donate food certificates. At times, the visitor may take the initiative to go shopping for basic foods, using the monetary gifts from a special parish fund.

Visiting with Pets

This project has become a welcome treat for residents in nursing homes or in assisted-living places. Children willingly share their pets for the purpose of entertaining the sick and elderly. After necessary screening, license approval, required supervision, and proper organization, pets are brought in and given to residents to hold or pet. It has been proven that contact with pet animals provides therapeutic help to shut-ins and often lifts them up from depression.

Sometimes toys or moveable objects are substituted for pets, including robotic dogs. Watching the various forms of movement that result from the touch of a dog, cat, or bird, or a battery-operated object not only brings amusement to the shut-ins, but also fills in the lonely spaces of their long days.

Knitting and Distributing Lap Blankets

Very often retired persons, elderly parishioners, or even shut-ins themselves look for something to occupy their minds and, at the same time, do good for others. If they are given scraps of yarn of various colors to knit lap blankets, they can make these useful gifts for patients in hospitals and nursing homes. These blankets are particularly welcome by those confined to wheelchairs. Placing a lap blanket over their legs protects them from the cold especially when they are transported outdoors. High school students are also capable of making and distributing lap blankets and often use this project as a special part of their service involvement for confirmation preparation.

Conversing with Photographs

Looking at photographs always awakens a connection to the particular events, times, and places where they were taken and becomes the source for wonderful conversations between the shut-in and the visitor. Photographs hold a special place in the memory of the homebound. Moreover, photos freeze time and help people recall specific occasions and happy times. Visitors are also encouraged to bring their personal photos to shut-ins so that they can share laughter and personal entertainment. Whether they are black and white or in color, small snapshots or in large frames, photos are a wonderful means of bringing enjoyment to shut-ins.

Entertaining with Art

Involvement in original art projects could include paintings, clay sculptures, seasonal novelties, crafts, or decorations of different kinds. Such projects have been found effective for reducing stress. At the same time, they bring a sense of empowerment for the homebound who are able to use their hands creatively.

When children engage in making masks of various sizes and shapes at Halloween, they can eagerly share them in the nursing homes and help to spark some pleasant conversations which in turn, can help release some hidden feelings. Seasonal decorations made with magnets, balloons, wind socks, and wreaths, as well as the construction of creative door hangers, also add to the cheerful atmosphere of shut-ins wherever they reside.

Connecting with CDs and Cassettes

A person who is homebound will need a CD player or cassette recorder in order to benefit from this type of sharing. Through this medium of communication shut-ins can listen to messages of cheer, inspiration, prayer, and instrumental or vocal music prepared specifically for them. Tapes may contain messages for a particular individual or for a group, and may include selected religious music for use during prayer gatherings in nursing homes. This type of service could be most beneficial to fill in some lonely hours with laughter and smiles, particularly when it includes voices of little children. It is a welcome gift to anyone, but is especially appreciated by those who live alone.

Assisting with Correspondence

Many persons who are homebound are unable to write notes on their own. Their unsteady hands and poor vision often hinder them in their attempts to correspond with others outside their residence. By helping them to write cards or answer their mail, they are given the opportunity to connect with persons dear to them. At times shut-ins at home are delinquent in paying their bills and would welcome another's assistance, particularly if the person is from the parish.

Designing Calendars

Too often shut-ins have difficulty keeping track of the days and dates in a week or month. By designing attractive calendars with large letters and numbers to hang on their wall, volunteers can help them connect with the present and also put them in touch with the dates and times of various events taking place in their community and parish.

Parading with Costumes

Seeing children dressed up in fancy attire always seems to be a treat for the sick and elderly no matter where they are. Watching children parade in costumes at Halloween, Thanksgiving, Christmas, Valentine's Day, St. Patrick's Day, or Easter brings special delight to them. Costumes may involve simply wearing a uniquely decorated hat or ribbon. Vocal or instrumental music enlivens the parade of children and ignites the spark of laughter and cheerful moods in this form of entertainment.

Constructing Place Mats

Whether used on individual trays or on tables in dining rooms, shut-ins will find delight in the decorated place mats which are made especially for them. Children of all ages can construct them and they may also be laminated for future use. The colors and pictures on them can reflect the particular season or feast being celebrated. Moreover, when place mats include various kinds of messages or puzzles on them, they become effective means for sharing conversations with others or helping an individual to pass the time in a thought-provoking activity.

Playing Games

Games that include cognitively stimulating activities and provoke self-expression (in a group or alone) can become powerful healing modalities for the shut-ins. They often become creative interruptions to their often very long and quiet days and are particularly welcome for distracting them from their chronic pain. Playing games not only allows people to become absorbed in mental concentration, but also enables players to enjoy camaraderie with one another. Hand-made or bought, games such as cards, checkers, marbles, bingo or puzzles, become an enjoyable pastime, and worth sharing with shut-ins anywhere.

Sharing Musical Talents

It has been demonstrated that music lowers blood pressure, reduces stress, and increases the body's chemistry to boost the immune system. Whether music is shared through the various instruments or through singing, it is sure to empower and facilitate interaction. It is a known fact that when sick and elderly residents listen to children or adults play instruments such as the piano, organ, accordion, or flute, or hear them sing popular songs familiar to them, emotions are released and spontaneous reactions emerge. A special dynamic is also evident when musical renditions include physical movement.

Performers who dance, tap feet, clap hands, and use body motions to the beat of their music, while inviting their audience to do likewise, are giving the shut-ins an opportunity for creative responses. Oftentimes, stroke victims or persons unable to speak have been found to release their emotions this way, and so are able to participate in the singing and bodily movement during such experiences. Indeed, music can allow persons to transcend their physical condition, taking them back to their previous form of life. And this type of sharing is always welcomed and encouraged. Moreover, music is a gift that not only benefits the listeners, but the performers as well.

Performing Miscellaneous Errands

There are a variety of errands which volunteers can do to benefit their sick and elderly members. Adults may offer to transport them to medical facilities, call on the telephone to check on their conditions, make appointments for them, shop for them, or perform personal tasks in their residence. Errands may also be performed by children who could show caring concern by raking leaves, shoveling snow, sweeping sidewalks, or emptying trash. Volunteers can share their willing hands and hearts wherever there is a need and in whatever manner assistance is welcomed.

Although these projects may not seem to require exceptional skills on the part of the volunteers, the cheerful involvement of the volunteers is an obvious demonstration of their genuine thoughtfulness and gentle compassion. Without ignoring the physical conditions of the sick and elderly, volunteers offer them a celebration of life and love in each of the forms of service. When volunteers provide the shut-ins with more opportunities for self-expression through their sharing of time and talent on their behalf, a form of healing always takes place. Compassionate care and genuine concern enables the homebound to broaden the scope of their environment.

The kinds of charitable activities listed here do not include every form of service which a parish may extend to their sick and elderly members, but, hopefully, these ideas will incite more participation and possibly provide ideas for new ways to share head-heart-hands with them in loving care.

CHAPTER SIX

Preparing the Volunteers

The ability to serve as a parish minister of care to the sick, disabled, and elderly demands some important considerations. The manner in which volunteers render service in this kind of ministry requires serious preparation, including prayerful attentiveness, careful deliberation, and dedicated commitment. However, Christian ministry involves more than serving God and the persons being ministered to in the parish. This service becomes a visible expression of the entire Church. It is the Church's living out of the gospel mandate to bring the healing power of Christ to its frail and aging members. Thus a volunteer must be willing to face honestly the challenges that arise in this ministry in the name of the Church at large.

Yet, there are limits to what a volunteer may or may not do and different approaches to follow for different circumstances. There are also times when support from others is necessary in order to continue to serve in this care-giving apostolate. Moreover, in addition to the periodic in-service programs which volunteers are asked to attend, they are encouraged to prepare for this ministry psychologically, prayerfully, and spiritually through retreats, spiritual reading, and participation in parish meetings.

Some of the practical hand-outs I have used to assist volunteers in their involvement include a combination of original reflections and a series of guidelines obtained from various resources. The comprehensive list of references, which is included at the end of the last chapter, was also made available for additional help.

The reflections and guidelines reprinted here were used in my introduction and preparation process for new parish ministers and for reinforcement with seasoned volunteers. It is hoped that in sharing this information, others might likewise find them useful in the training of new volunteers for the ministry to their sick and aged parishioners.

Recommendations for Bringing the Eucharist

1. Pray before you visit the shut-in.

2. Call before going to the home.

3. Bring the Project H.E.A.L. manual of prayers.

4. Share prayer and Scripture before giving Communion.

5. Do not be concerned about the person's eating schedule. The sick and elderly do not need to adhere to the rules for fasting.

6. The homebound sick may need water. Be alert to their needs.

7. Do not be in a hurry to leave.

8. Be reverent and share prayer after giving Communion.

9. Share news of the parish; bring them the latest bulletin.

10. Do not add new people to your list without notifying the coordinator.

Some Dos and Don'ts

• You determine how much time you can give to the person you visit. We suggest a weekly visit on the day and for the length of time that is agreeable to both of you.

• In the beginning, do not give out your phone number if you do not wish your privacy to be intruded upon. As you grow more comfortable in your relationship, you may arrange to connect regularly and decide to give out your number.

• Be careful to do only what you choose to do. Once a precedent is established, it will be difficult to change it.

• It is best to begin with limited activities, then you may do more if you wish.

• Never accept money or gifts of intrinsic value. It may create problems with the person's family.

• Keep the situation of the person, and personal, medical, financial, or family issues confidential.

• Be prepared for emergencies (911) and have the numbers of relatives or close friends handy.

• Do not discuss your problems. You are there to uplift. Do share joyful things about your life.

Adapted from *Friendly Visitors Training and Resource Manual: Breakthrough to the Aging*

Caring

To care does not simply mean to be nice and congenial to a shut-in. Rather, as Henri Nouwen and Walter Gaffney assert in their book, *Aging,*

> To care one must offer one's own vulnerable self to others as a source of healing To care for the aging, for instance, means first of all to enter into close contact with your own aging self, to sense your time, and to experience the movements of your own life cycle.

Caring enables persons to be in partnership for a specific purpose. The focus of that partnership is for sharing genuine concern, for offering positive assistance, and for building up one another in body, mind, and spirit.

When we care, we bear another's burdens, mindful of our connection as brothers and sisters in Christ who are part of the same body in the family of God.

A Care-Giver's Prayer

Dear Lord,
thank you for the privilege of sharing your compassionate love
in a special way with _____(name),
whom you have called me to assist.

Although it is not always easy to respond to his (her) needs
as promptly as I would like,
your grace allows me to bring your healing presence
where otherwise, much loneliness and sadness would prevail.

I praise you for this call
to be your instrument of hope and peace.
Bless me with continued strength
to fulfill this mission with which you have entrusted me,
and help me to bring the healing joy of your Holy Spirit
through all that I am and do.
I ask this through Christ, Our Lord. Amen.

Skills for the Care-Giver

1. Find out pertinent information about the person to be contacted from the pastor or coordinator.

2. Read the appropriate care-cards.

3. Call and make an appointment for the visit, if appropriate.

4. Think about the person to be contacted. Consider the kinds of things that person may be thinking or feeling.

5. Listen with acceptance to the person.

6. Use open-ended questions.

7. Be aware of the feelings present.

8. Avoid the temptation to solve someone else's problem.

9. Do not debate or invalidate the feelings of the person.

United Church of Christ, *Called to Care Pocket Handbook*

Hints while Sharing Scripture

- During your pastoral visit, offer to share Scripture with the person.

- Invite him or her to select personal preferences of Scripture passages.

- Use a translation of the Bible that is suitable for you and the shut-in.

- Choose Scripture verses that focus on healing and on uplifting the spirit.

- Respect the responses of the shut-in and avoid lengthy reflections.

- Conclude the Scripture reading with prayer.

The following prayer or a similar one can be made into a card and distributed to parishioners who were newly admitted patients in the hospital to encourage them and let them know of the loving concern and prayer of the parish community:

> Dear Friend,
> You are in our loving thoughts
> and in our special prayer.
> Accept this little greeting,
> a sign of heartfelt care.
> May you feel God's healing hand
> bring strength to you today,
> And may the Holy Spirit
> forever bless your way!

Ten Reminders for the Pastoral Care Team

1. It is more important to know the person than the disease.

2. A friendly environment cuts recovery time in half. Be cheerful!

3. The touch of kindness brings healing. A stern approach creates set-backs.

4. Never make negative or judgmental comments to the shut-in.

5. Encourage a sense of hope, even when the person's condition is chronic.

6. Respect the patient's rights and needs concerning doctors, medications, and treatments.

7. Not only medical professionalism, but also gentle compassion and reassurance, help the sick.

8. Infirm persons are not all in the same physical, emotional, or spiritual state. Treat them as individuals.

9. Keep everything about the patient in strictest confidence.

10. God's healing power flows through our prayer and acts of love, patience, and gentleness. Consider it a privilege to serve in this healing ministry!

Guidelines for Eucharistic Ministry in Healthcare Facilities

1. Eucharistic ministers are to observe all archdiocesan and parish directives regarding distribution of the Eucharist outside of Mass.

2. Holy Communion is to be given only to Catholics who are disposed to receive this sacrament.

3. If a patient or resident would like to receive the sacrament of reconciliation prior to the reception of the Eucharist, you should notify the parish priest.

4. If a communicant faces difficulty in swallowing, the Eucharistic Minister should use proper discretion to break the sacred Host into a particle that facilitates the reception of Communion. If necessary, water should be available.

5. The healthcare facility personnel should make available to the parish two lists:

     a. a list of all Catholic residents who will receive Communion

     b. a list of all parishioners of the parish, for their records

6. All Catholic residents capable of participating in the Communion Service in the facility should be transported to the designated room for the communal prayer. They will receive Holy Communion during this service.

7. Holy Communion will be brought to individuals only when their physical condition does not allow them to leave their rooms.

8. When the Eucharist is brought to individual rooms, the television or radio should be turned off, out of reverence and respect for the divine Presence.

9. Non-Catholic Christians should never be given the Eucharist. (Please refer to the directives which explain archdiocesan norms regarding Intercommunion.)

10. A priest should be notified for bringing Eucharist and anointing of the sick to Catholics who are in a seriously ill condition and desire to receive the sacraments. The family or persons responsible for contacting the priests should encourage the reception of the sacraments while the patients are still aware of the sacramental rite. They should not wait until the patient is at the death-bed stage of his or her condition. The sacraments are for the living, not for the deceased.

Eight Beatitudes for Those who Minister to the Sick and Elderly

Blessed are you who listen to your patients,

especially those with constant complaints,

for you possess the ears of Christ.

Blessed are you who see the hurts of your patients,

especially those overlooked by others,

for you possess the eyes of Christ.

Blessed are you who speak kindly to your patients,

especially those plagued by fear and anger,

for you possess the mouth of Christ.

Blessed are you who touch your patients gently,

especially those bruised by insensitivity,

for you possess the hands of Christ.

Blessed are you who think prayerfully of your patients,

especially those alone and discouraged,

for you possess the mind of Christ.

Blessed are you who show love to your patients,

especially those with chronic illness,

for you possess the heart of Christ.

Blessed are you who walk tirelessly to your patients,

especially those with repeated calls,

for you possess the feet of Christ.

Blessed are you who persevere in your ministry,

especially with compassion to all patients,

for you possess the healing presence of Christ,

and yours is the kingdom of heaven.

Parish Hospital Ministry

The purpose of this ministry is to enable volunteers to assist the staff at a hospital in their efforts to provide spiritual support to Catholics who are admitted to this hospital. Under the direction of the volunteer service coordinator or another individual, volunteers engage in the following services:

1. Consult hospital officials to learn which patients have requested the reception of the sacrament of the Eucharist.

2. Make available the list of these patients for the eucharistic ministers on the days they bring communion to the patients.

3. Instruct the eucharistic ministers to refer to the nurses' stations on each floor to verify each patient's capability for receiving communion.

4. Assist the staff in notifying the parish of a patient's admission to the hospital if he/she agrees to make this known to the parish priests or their representatives.

5. Be a contact person for notifying the parish of any concerns that need to be addressed, such as requests for the sacrament of reconciliation and the sacrament of the anointing of the sick.

6. Uphold in strictest confidentiality each patient's hospital stay and physical condition.

7. Be a source of healing inspiration to those you encounter through your involvement as volunteers in this ministry of care at the hospital.

What to Say?

What to say to seriously ill persons is probably the greatest concern for individuals who plan to visit critically sick people at their residences, in the hospital, or in a nursing home. Often the visitor may think that he/she must be equipped with special answers for any complex question posed by the sick.

Those who are extremely ill, however, look more for visitors who can listen with love and who will allow them to speak without judgment and without restraint. Reflective, sensitive listening becomes a key and an invaluable skill for the visitor.

In his book *Together By Your Side*, Joseph Champlin states that there are two basic steps involved in reflective listening:

1. Really hearing and understanding what the other person is saying through words and body language.

2. Reflecting the feelings and thoughts you heard through your own words, tone of voice, body posture and gestures so that the other person knows that he or she is understood.

Other practical steps in reflective listening should include:

• creating a climate that encourages non-threatening invitations to talk

• respecting the privacy of one's choice to disclose feelings

• observing and accepting non-verbal communication such as movement of eyes, hand gestures, or facial expressions

• making statements that show caring compassion and understanding especially during someone's outburst or display of tearful emotions

• allowing ample time for communication and taking into consideration questions of concern or signs of apprehension

• avoiding negative comments that could lessen open dialogue or freedom of expression.

Listen

When I ask you to listen to me and you start giving advice,
you have not done what I asked.

When I ask you to listen to me and you begin to tell me
why I shouldn't feel that way,
you are trampling on my feelings.

When I ask you to listen to me and you feel you have to do
something to solve my problems,
you have failed me, strange as that may seem.

Listen! All I asked was that you listen, not talk to or do,
just hear me.
Advice is cheap; you can get both Dear Abby
and Billy Graham in the same newspaper.

And I can do for myself; I am not helpless;
maybe discouraged and faltering, but not helpless.
When you do something for me that I can and need to do for myself,
you contribute to my fear and weakness.

But when you accept as a simple fact that I do feel
what I feel, no matter how irrational, then I can quit
trying to convince you and can get about the business
of understanding what's behind this irrational feeling.
And when that's clear, the answers are obvious
and I don't need advice. Irrational feelings make sense
when we understand what's behind them.

So, please listen and just hear me.
And, if you want to talk, wait a minute for your turn;
and I'll listen to you.

— *Anonymous*

CHAPTER SEVEN

Introducing Shut~Ins to Spiritual Resources

There is a natural tendency for those who face pain or suffering to seek freedom or relief from their harsh realities. But when the condition becomes chronic, or shows no visible sign of even a slight change, a feeling of resentment or bitterness may overtake them and even prompt a serious questioning of faith or trust in God. A lack of confidence or hope in life may also lead to isolation and depression. Yet, Jesus has shown power over suffering and death not by taking it away, but by filling it with his healing presence.

Through prayer and meditation, it is possible for an individual to endure the difficulties of sickness or old age by uniting their suffering with the crucified Christ on the cross. In prayer, suffering can be transformed into something of value. Bishop Sheen once said: "The tragedy of suffering is that so much of it is wasted." Hence it is in the times of steadfast prayer where true strength is gained for accepting and surrendering pain and suffering as God's holy will. Prayer also leads us to realize that pain can drive us beyond the world of self-pity in order to reach out and embrace others.

As Cardinal Newman prayed: "God has created me to do some definite service. I have my mission. If I am in sickness, my sickness may serve him, in perplexity, my perplexity may serve him. If I am in sorrow, my sorrow may serve him. He does nothing in vain. He knows what he is about. Therefore, I will trust him." By uniting in prayer and invoking God's healing power, we can gain strength and peace for ourselves and for others. We can unite in solidarity with others who face similar physical, spiritual, or mental suffering.

In addition to the powerhouse of prayer, a connection can be made with others who might be suffering in related ways. Certain organizations link people through the medium of personal correspondence in a network of spiritual resources. Various religious affiliations invite the sick, disabled, and elderly to join them as members so that they need not travel their route of pain alone. These sources bond them together for the purpose of establishing a prayer network among them and for enabling them to lend support to other sick, disabled, and elderly members. Members share and receive encouragement, prayer, and support in their similar conditions.

I have acquired a list of some of these spiritual resources and organizations, along with their addresses and a brief description of their objectives.

1. *Uplift*, a monthly newsletter for handicapped people. Focuses on ways to energize and engage persons for actively pursuing a spiritual relationship with God through prayer, study, and worship.

> Victory Missionaries
> National Shrine of Our Lady of Snows
> 9500 West III, Rt. 15
> Belleville, Illinois 62223

2. *Care Notes: Strength and Help for a Friend*
Hope Notes: Help and Healing for Heart and Soul
Prayer Notes: Letting Illness Bring You Closer to God
These small booklets give help to those coping with difficulties in body, mind, and spirit; to help find God's healing power when feeling broken and helpless. Various topics are written by authors who are experts in the areas of spiritual, physical, psychological services. These notes offer a blend of information and inspiration, modern psychology, and religion, and are available by subscribing through Abbey Press.

> One Caring Place
> Abbey Press
> St. Meinrad, Indiana 47577

3. *C.U.S.A.*: Catholics United for Spiritual Action (Formerly known as Catholic Union of the Sick in America) This is an organization of Catholics whose state of health is occasion for sacrifice. An active apostolate which unites its chronically ill or disabled members in the Cross of Christ. Membership consists of poor and rich, laity and religious, all united in the common bond of suffering and love, and whose aim is to help each other and others as well. CUSANs are united through group-letters or a cassette group tape which regularly brings news of the other members of the group and a message from the group's spiritual advisor. Each CUSAN adds a message to the group-letter or tape and mails it to the next group member. Members strive to unite the lonely and forgotten who may be relegated to back rooms or out of sight so they can be brought into the light of hope and love again.

CUSA teaches through example, that pain accepted with patience and trust in God has tremendous power for the salvation of souls. "We suffer with a purpose" is their theme. They learn that they are not useless or unproductive people because they are bedridden, blind, deaf, or paralyzed.

> CUSA
> 176 West 8th Street
> Bayonne, New Jersey 07002

4. *The Caring Community* (monthly subscription). the goal of this periodical is to connect the homebound and hospitalized to the faith community. Eucharistic ministers and other pastoral ministers can carry this monthly newsletter with them to use as a special focus during visits, or they can be received in the mail. This newsletter includes an introduction to the Sunday readings, a conversational essay which ties the readings to the spirituality of everyday life, and prayer starters to encourage readers to reach out to others in prayer.

> *The Caring Community*
> Celebration Publications
> P.O. Box 419493
> Kansas City, Missouri 64141-6493

5. *Living with Christ.* This monthly publication enables shut-ins to follow the Mass on television with the readings proper to each Sunday. Pastoral visitors can drop off *Living with Christ* each month. This is a great way to help your shut-ins feel connected to Sunday and daily Mass, and to the parish they love. Along with the full texts of both the Sunday and the daily Mass readings, *Living with Christ* offers the prayers of the liturgy, brief biographies of the saints, morning an evening prayer formulas, and additional thoughts for spiritual inspiration and support.

> Novalis-Bayard
> 185 Willow Street
> PO Box 6001
> Mystic, CT 06355

6. *Christopher News Notes.* Uses the printed word to spread two basic ideas: "There's nobody like you." and "You can make a difference." Based on the Judeo-Christian concept of service to God and all humanity, their motto is: "Better to light one candle than to curse the darkness." These News Notes are distributed monthly and include reflections to ponder on regarding life's many realities.

> The Christophers
> 12 East 48th Street
> New York, New York 10017

7. *Stauros Notebook: Reflections on the Mystery of Suffering.* A four-page leaflet printed every two months, this international, ecumenical organization promotes studies and programs on specific areas of human suffering from a religious point of view, particularly from a Christian perspective."Stauros" is a Greek word for "Cross"—the Christian symbol which proclaims the belief that all suffering has special meaning and worth through the death and resurrection of Jesus Christ.

> Stauros International
> Catholic Theological Union
> 5401 S. Cornell Avenue
> Chicago, Illinois 60615

8. The Christian Fraternity of the Sick (founded in Verdun, France in 1942). This organization offers a ministry to the sick by the sick; they are called to carry the sign of the cross in their bodies and the joy of the resurrection in their hearts. The invitation of the Suffering Servant is a call

to heal others even while we ourselves are wounded. It is the challenge to empty ourselves of our own desires and needs and give ourselves in service to our fellow sufferers.

This apostolic movement is based on evangelical charity, which opens the door to almost any kind of sharing. The movement was introduced in Peru in 1967 by a dynamic Jesuit, Padre Manual Duato, who won for himself the nickname, "Padre Quitapenas"—the priest who takes away pain. His own experience of physical pain, coupled with a joyous spirit, made him the kind of suffering servant who calls others forth to a new way of life. The prayer of this fraternity follows:

Prayer of the Suffering Servant

We do not ask that you return our sight,
but we do ask that you open the eyes of
our society to discover the true values of
justice, love, and peace.
We do not ask that you give us back our legs,
but we do ask that our brothers and sisters walk united toward you.
We do not ask that you restore our hands,
but we do ask that you teach all that there is
more joy in giving than in receiving, and that
fraternity is sharing everything as you have done with us.
We do not ask that you raise us from our beds,
but we do ask that you give us the strength
to touch the hearts of those who have given up,
who do not believe in the Light. Amen.

• Sister Patricia Lowery, M.M. (*Liguorian,* February, 1980)

9. The Apostolate of Suffering/ Auxiliary League of the Enthronement of the Sacred Heart in the Home. Tears shed without love are wasted and embitter the soul. To weep with love consoles, sanctifies and redeems. Members are asked to offer every day their pains, sufferings, disappointments, and hardships for the glory of God. Their daily prayer includes this prayer to the Sacred Heart:

Most Sacred Heart of Jesus,
through the Immaculate and Sorrowful Heart of Mary,
I offer you the treasure of all my physical and mental sufferings,
and I praise and thank you, O King of Love, in all my sorrows,
asking in exchange the extension of your reign.
May your kingdom come by your Cross and my crosses!
Sacred Heart of Jesus, your kingdom come!

Apostolate of Suffering
Sacred Heart Center
P.O.Box 39191
Louisville, Kentucky 40233

10. The Ministry of Praise is founded on the convictions of the power of prayer, and the need of the elderly, homebound, and handicapped to know that they play an important role in the parish. Countless people suffer from feelings of uselessness or isolation from their parish. This ministry attempts to remedy that and, at the same time, enhance its members' spiritual lives and bring blessings upon the whole community. The Ministry of Praise can be the spiritual lifeline of a parish and gives the shut-in a sense of participation in the life and work of the Church. Members receive a wooden cross, a certificate confirming their ministry, and a prayer book.

> Sr. Mary Charla Gannon, R.S.M.
> St. Bede the Venerable Church
> 8200 S. Kostner Avenue
> Chicago, Illinois 60652

11. *Ministering to Persons with Mental Illness and their Families.* This newsletter helps people understand and support those suffering from mental illness. It offers a Christian approach to ministering with the mentally ill, as well as offers reading lists and reflections on various issues confronted by mentally ill persons. References are provided with addresses and phone numbers of people for contact and support.

> Editors: J.R. Breton (3 Apple Tree Lane, Walpole, MA 02081)
> Rev. Scott Dow (P.O.Box 724, Augusta, ME 04332)
> Publisher: William Stubbs (69 Caron St., Portland, ME 04103)

12. *Good News NEWS* (where all the students are seniors). The goal of this publication is to bring authentic Church teaching to older Catholics in a changing world. St. Thomas Aquinas Society's bimonthly newsletter is under the direction of the University of St. Thomas. Personal contact through one-on-one correspondence—supportive and confidential—is offered on a continuing basis by priests. Full membership is available for $20.

> Society of St. Thomas Aquinas
> University of St. Thomas
> P.O. Box 65346
> St. Paul, Minnesota 55164

13. Apostolate of Prayer for the Sick. The goal of this group is to bring loved ones closer to God in their suffering through the Sacred Heart League. Members are asked to do three things:

> 1. Consecrate their sickness to the Sacred Heart of Jesus by placing his picture at their bedside.
> 2. Pray the offering prayer with them, or for them if they are not able.
> 3. Through the sacrifice of the Mass, daily offer their suffering and their pain to God in union with Christ's own suffering.
> Write to:
> Sacred Heart League
> Walls, Mississippi 38686

14. *How a Christian Can Cope with Chronic Pain,* by Father Basil Pennington, is based on recommendations from the American Chronic Pain Association. He borrows from the ten-step pro-

gram that ACPA suggests to live with chronic pain and makes it a twelve-step process. The steps for moving "from patient to person" bear a Christian approach and are as follows:

1. Acceptance of pain

2. Getting involved

3. Priorities

4. Realistic goals

5. We know our basic rights

6. Recognize emotions

7. Relaxation

8. Exercise

9. Attitude

10. Outreach

11. With Christ

12. Centering Prayer

More information on pain management is available by contacting the ACP Association.
American Chronic Pain Association
257 Old Haymaker Rd.
Monroeville, Pennsylvania 15146 (412-856-9676)

15. *Meditations for the Sick, Aging and Homebound.* This pamphlet provides prayerful reflection to shut-ins and encourages the practice of the words of Pope Paul VI: "Here is something big and new; suffering is no longer useless. If united to Christ's pains, our pain takes on something of his expiatory power, of his redemptive power, of his saving power." This booklet includes a reflection, a petition, a Scripture passage and a practice.
Franciscan Mission Associates
280 West Lincoln Avenue
Mount Vernon, New York 10550

16. St. Peregrine Prayer Society. St. Peregrine is considered the patron saint of cancer victims and this society attempts to minister to persons with cancer, in compassionate sensitivity, prayer, and mutual support. Through a monthly newsletter, reflective thoughts and testimonies by those who have been healed of their cancer are shared with members. They pray daily this prayer to St. Peregrine:

Prayer to St. Peregrine

Dear St. Peregrine, I need your help. I feel so uncertain of my life right now. This serious illness makes me long for a sign of God's love. Help me imitate your enduring faith when you faced the ugliness of cancer and surgery. Allow me to trust the Lord the way you did in this moment of distress. I want to be cured, but right now I ask God for the strength to bear the cross in my life. I seek the power to proclaim God's presence in my life despite the hardship, anguish, and fear I now experience. O Glorious St. Peregrine, be an inspiration to me and a petitioner of these needed graces from our loving Father. Amen.

Write to:
St. Peregrine Prayer Society
P.O. Box 211
Notre Dame, Indiana 46556

17. *A Prayer for Vocations* can be used to offer special prayer for an increase of religious vocations of priests, brothers, and sisters in the world. The following prayers are recommended for daily recitation by the sick and elderly and are available upon request:

A Prayer of the Sick for Vocations

Lord, you know my condition.

You know my sickness and pain.

You know too, Lord, the hurt and pain of all the world.

Your healing presence is shown in a special way

through the lives of priests, brothers, and sisters.

But we need many, many more.

We need priests, brothers and sisters to visit the sick

to cherish the elderly,

to comfort the dying,

to be with the poor and suffering

to teach in our schools,

to be compassionate and sincere, loving and holy.

Call many young men and women today, Lord.

Share with them your concern for us.

Share with them your healing love,

that they might know it in their lives

and share it with all the people they touch.

Call many young men and women today, O Lord. Amen.

A Senior Citizen's Prayer for Vocations

Lord, I have spent many days on your earth.

Many priests, brothers, and sisters have crossed my path.

Priests married my children, baptized my grandchildren.

They assisted on my Confirmation Day and shared the joy of my First Holy Communion.

Sisters and brothers visited me when I was sick, taught my children in school.

Today, we need many more priests, sisters and brothers to continue your work on earth.

O Lord, speak loudly to this generation, that some might respond to your call.

Give these your people a vision, your vision.

Make them compassionate and sincere.

Make them men and women of the gospel and good counselors of your people.

Make them holy men and women, Lord,

with the wisdom of the aged, and the vision of the young.

Lord, hear this ancient cry. Amen.

For more information on these prayers, write to:
Vocation Center
230 Genesee Street
Trenton, New Jersey 08611

18. *Reflective Whisperings: Prayer Poems.* These prayers, some of which appear earlier in this book, are whisperings of God's love in times of sickness and pain. They help people who are experiencing difficulties due to sickness and pain to reflect upon God's gifts of healing strength and hope. This booklet of twenty prayer poems is a reflective aid for inspiring renewed faith in God through gentle whisperings of hope, trust and love. Each prayer poem includes a reminder that God's unconditional love and care surround us in every circumstance of our life.

The prayer poems are available on single cards or in booklet form and may be obtained by writing to:

Sr. Marie Roccapriore, M.P.F.
St. Thomas Convent
20 Eden Place
Southington, Connecticut 06489

19. *The Sacrament of the Anointing of the Sick and the Elderly*. This pamphlet is also written by Sr. Marie Roccapriore and is available from the address above (#18). It includes a concise description of the sacrament along with answers to these common questions:

- Why do we have a sacramental anointing?

- What takes place in the Rite of Anointing?

- Who can receive the sacrament?

- Can this sacrament be received more than once?

- Where do celebrations of the anointing take place?

- What happens at a communal celebration of the Anointing of the Sick?

In addition to providing positive information to individuals, this pamphlet can be distributed to the entire parish as a bulletin insert, or given out at a communal Anointing of the Sick.

CHAPTER EIGHT

Information & Tips for the Parish

The following samples of letters, notes, and bulletin inserts are shared here to offer some help in the planning phases of the various events surrounding the ministry to the sick and elderly in the parish. Permission is given by the publisher to reproduce these for non-commercial use within a parish. You can adapt them as needed for your group.

Project H.E.A.L. Mission Statement

Jesus invites us to extend his healing ministry by showing compassion to those suffering in mind and body. We strive to respond to this invitation by recognizing the needs of our sick and elderly parishioners through a ministry of care. This parish outreach will engage volunteers (children and adults) to share their presence, prayer, and deeds with them through sacramental, spiritual, and charitable forms of service. Project H.E.A.L. is a parish ministry of care that strives to make the Homebound Encouraged through Assistance in Love.

Memo: To All Members of Project H.E.A.L.

From: _____ (coordinator of parish ministry of care)

Re: Invitation to participate in the sacramental anointing liturgy

On Sunday, _____ (date), our parish will celebrate the sacramental Anointing of the Sick and the Elderly at the _____ (time) Mass. As a member of our parish ministry of care, Project H.E.A.L., you are invited to participate in this liturgical celebration. Along with the medical personnel, you are invited to take part in the procession and be seated in the pew reserved for you. We ask that you arrive at the church by _____ (time).

We plan to host a reception in the hall immediately following the Mass, and welcome any help you would be willing to give. We need assistance to:

- set up the hall on Saturday afternoon at 1:30 p.m.
- bring baked items, finger foods, or fruit
- serve at the reception
- clean up after the reception.

Please call_____ (phone number) if you are able to attend this Mass and also if you are able to offer help in any of the above-mentioned areas.

God bless you for your dedication in ministering to our sick and elderly in the nursing homes, hospitals, or in their homes! In their name and in the name of the entire parish, we thank you and prayerfully acknowledge your wonderful involvement. You are indeed, extending the healing mission of Jesus.

Important Reminders Concerning the Liturgy of the Anointing of the Sick

Distribute badges to those being anointed. (Candidates need not be separated from loved ones.) Check attendance of those registered.

1. Every other pew should be empty to allow priests the freedom to move about during the silent laying on of hands and also during the actual anointing.

2. At Communion priests will go to those who are not ambulatory. Those receiving Communion need not move from their pews. Simply extend the hands as you normally receive Eucharist in the hands. We ask that anyone who has difficulty walking sit in one of the front pews on either side.

3. The names of all being anointed today will be carried up at the Preparation of Gifts and placed on the altar. (See basket.)

4. We encourage everyone to follow the Anointing Rite on page __ of the worship aid.

5. The Anointing Rite takes place after the homily of the Mass. The priest will come to the pews to lay hands on all who will be anointed (those wearing badges). If possible, you are asked to kneel while those not being anointed remain seated. Otherwise, remain in a comfortable position.

6. The priest will come around again to anoint the sick and elderly with oil on the forehead and the palm of each hand. As he anoints the forehead, he offers a prayer to which we respond: "Amen"; as he anoints the hands, he offers another prayer to which we respond again: "Amen."

7. Our children's music ministry will join us at this Mass to share their singing. Their special ministry is to reach out to the sick and the elderly through their music.

8. There are nurses and doctors among our parishioners who have offered to share their presence at this Mass and are seated in the rear of the church. If anyone needs to connect with them during the Mass, feel free to do so. We are grateful to them for joining us at this celebration.

Sharing Time and Talent

Are you retired? Do you have time to share your presence with another? Would you like to become involved in bringing joy to persons who are sick or elderly? Perhaps this parish project is for you.

One of the great challenges Christians face today is the acceptance of opportunities to share time and talent with others without thought of personal gain or remuneration. Yet, Christ himself reminds us of this challenge over and over in the gospels. He spent his entire public life healing and tending to others in need with his compassionate love.

In response to the challenge of meeting needs of the elderly and sick in our faith community, and in light of the recommendations set forth by the archdiocese to implement the stewardship process in our parish, we are seeking volunteers to be part of a special Ministry of Care, Project H.E.A.L., that will offer to our Homebound Encouragement through Assistance in Love. This outreach would include sharing prayer, presence, and performance through spiritual and charitable dimensions of service.

Too often, persons who at one time were visibly active and productive in society or church communities have become isolated, neglected, and forgotten because of sickness or old age. The goal of this ministry is to gain a greater awareness of the state of our homebound parishioners, to recognize their tremendous spiritual contribution to the Church, and to provide opportunities that would allow them to experience closer ties with our parish family.

We ask any child or adult to consider seriously and prayerfully how you might share some of your personal time and talent in this aspect of service.

If you are willing to give service in this ministry or would like more information, please call_____ (phone number and contact name).

Letter to Parishioners Inviting Them to Project H.E.A.L.

Dear Parishioner,

One of the great challenges Christians face today is the acceptance of opportunities to share time and talent with others without thought of personal gain or remuneration. Yet, Christ himself reminds us of this challenge over and over in the gospels. He spent his entire public life healing and tending to others in need with his compassionate love.

In response to the challenge of meeting needs of the elderly and the sick in our faith community, our parish is in the process of forming a special Ministry of Care called Project H.E.A.L. (Homebound Encouraged through Assistance in Love). This outreach would include sacramental, spiritual, and charitable dimensions of service to them.

So often, persons who at one time were visibly active and productive in society or church communities have become isolated, neglected, and forgotten because of sickness or old age. One of the aspects of this ministry of care is to make people aware of the condition of our homebound parishioners and also of their tremendous contribution to our Church. Our aim is to help the homebound experience being part of our parish family. Project H.E.A.L. includes a wide range of involvement and we invite anyone (child or adult) to participate in this Ministry of Care. We ask you to consider seriously and prayerfully how you might share some of your time and talent in this worthwhile project of service to our sick and elderly parishioners.

Areas of Involvement in Project H.E.A.L.:

A. *Sacramental.* This aspect is covered by priests, deacons, or eucharistic ministers and includes the sacraments of reconciliation and anointing of sick (offered by a priest) and Eucharist (offered by a priest, deacon, or eucharistic minister).

B. *Spiritual.* Visits or contacts are of a spiritual nature and can include:

    1. Prayer-line

    2. Shared prayer

    3. Rosary

    4. Religious tapes

    5. Scripture reading

    6. Inspirational books/cards

    7. Children's Music Ministry: Spirit Joy

    8. Other_____

C. *Charitable.* Involvement may take place weekly or occasionally and can include:

    1. Friendly visitation (home, hospital, nursing home)

    2. Telephone reassurance

    3. Performing miscellaneous errands

    4. Sending greeting cards (on birthdays, holidays, etc.)

    5. Making various favors, novelties, crafts, etc.

    6. Inviting someone who lives alone into your home to share a meal with your family occasionally.

    7. Baking cookies to share with the homebound

    8. Arranging flowers and plants specifically for the sick and elderly

Please fill in the information below and return to the parish office. You will be contacted soon after we receive your reply. Thank you!

Yes, I wish to participate in our Parish Ministry of Care: Project H.E.A.L.

Name_____

Address_____

City_____State_____Zip_____

Telephone_____

E-mail_____

Please list area(s) of involvement you would like to commit yourself to. Feel free to add any suggestions.

_____

Letter to Parishioners Inviting Them to Project H.E.A.L. (Short version)

One of the great challenges Christians face today is the acceptance of opportunities to share time and talent with others without thought of personal gain or remuneration. Yet, Christ himself reminds us of our obligation to do so. The gospels tell us that Jesus spent his entire public life healing and tending to others in need with his compassionate love.

In response to the challenge of meeting needs in our faith community, our parish is in the process of forming a special ministry of care. This outreach would include involvement of a sacramental, spiritual, and charitable nature. The main focus of this ministry is to make people aware of our caring concern for them and, at the same time, allow them to experience being part of our parish family.

We ask you to consider prayerfully how you might share some of your time and talent with our Parish Ministry of Care. If you would like more information, please contact _____(name).

Please fill in the information below and return to the parish office. You will be contacted soon after we receive your reply. Thank you!

Yes, I wish to participate in our Parish Ministry of Care: Project H.E.A.L.

Name_____

Address_____

City_____State_____Zip_____

Telephone_____

E-mail_____

Please list area(s) of involvement you would like to commit yourself to. Feel free to add any suggestions.

For the bulletin

Attention!

The third week of May (add dates) is designated "A Week to Remember the Elderly and Disabled Shut-ins" in a special way. Parishioners are being asked to consider sharing some time, talent, and service with these brothers and sisters in a particular way during this week.

Members of our Parish Ministry of Care, Project H.E.A.L., are already committed to this kind of involvement. They visit homebound parishioners, and hospitals, bringing the Eucharist and sharing prayer and cheerful smiles. Children in our parish school are also extending themselves to share with these people through various kinds of creative projects. We invite everyone in the parish to set aside a little time to reach out and touch someone who is elderly, sick, or disabled in gentle compassion through a visit, a creative activity, a letter, a card, or in any other manner that might bring the homebound the healing hope and love of Jesus. Perhaps you are retired, or at home during the day and are looking for something to do to help others. We invite you to consider involvement in this outreach of compassionate concern and care.

If anyone would like to join our Parish Project H.E.A.L. Team or would like to have more information on how to help reach out to shut-ins, or could share ideas on more ways to participate in this healing ministry, please feel free to contact _____(phone and contact name).

Parish Advent Project

The Giving Tree

As Christmas approaches, we prepare ourselves in many ways to celebrate this beautiful feast. We decorate our homes, buy gifts for family and friends, send Christmas cards, or bake various kinds of cookies, cakes, or pies. But no matter how we choose to anticipate this sacred event, without doubt a great deal of time and money surround our preparations. We Christians, however, should be aware of the many people who have less than we have, even to the point of lacking essentials such as food, clothing, and shelter.

During the next few weeks our parish family will be involved in a special Advent project called the Giving Tree. Each of us is invited to remember needy people by sharing gifts and placing them under the tree located in our church.

To participate in this Advent project, simply purchase one or more of the gifts suggested on this paper (include Christmas paper and ribbon but please do not wrap), and place them under the Giving Tree. The gifts must be new and unused.

For every gift you place under the tree, place a paper "gift circle" on the tree. (Gift circles are in the basket near the tree.) If you bring three gifts, place three "gift circles" on the tree. This will help us as a parish community to see our tree transformed into a special Gift Sharing Tree by Christmas.

Before Christmas, we will distribute the gifts to needy persons in the community, to the sick and elderly who are homebound and in convalescent centers. The gifts are for men, women, teens, children and infants. Some suggested gifts are:

Mittens, Scarves, Gloves, Socks, Slippers, Underwear, Sweat Shirts, Sheets, Blankets, Winter Hats, Robes, Night Gowns, Pajamas, Lotions, Powder, Food Certificates, Toys, Games, Candy, Jewelry

Please remember that your gift must be new and unused, and that all gifts should be placed under the Giving Tree no later than December 16. If you have any questions pertaining to this project, feel free to call _____(contact person and phone number).

Thank you for your generosity. May God bless you!

Project H.E.A.L Parish Ministry of Care
Important Reminders to Eucharistic Ministers

1. As a Minister of the Eucharist, you should be properly dressed while serving in your role as bearer of Holy Communion to the shut-in parishioners, whether they are at home, in the hospital or in a nursing home.

2. Our parish conducts special services in the healthcare facilities, according to the manual prepared by the liturgical commission of the Archdiocese. Please adhere to these directives.

3. The team leader for each nursing home represents the parish and should be contacted directly if you are unable to participate on your scheduled day.

4. The parish coordinator is responsible for all communication between the parish and the nursing home, and will handle all changes in schedule or cancellation of services.

5. Two Project H.E.A.L. cards must be completed for every homebound parishioner you visit. One is maintained by you; the other is kept in the rectory. The person who coordinates the homebound ministry will be responsible for the accurate recording and revised information on the cards and will notify you of any changes.

6. Please record on the cards all the dates of your visits to the parishioners and include any helpful comments that will provide us with ideas for extending more care to them.

7. During your visit, if you come to learn of others who are not on the parish list, but who could also benefit from this ministry, notify the coordinator immediately.

8. Remember to ask about the celebration of the sacraments of reconciliation and anointing. The parish priests will gladly visit to offer these sacraments.

9. A parish greeting card to the sick is available for distribution to parishioners in hospitals, homes, and healthcare facilities. Kindly obtain them from the rectory office and leave with the shut-ins during your visit.

10. Share the spiritual resources suggested for shut-ins and encourage them to join in a ministry that recommends offering their sufferings in prayer and solidarity with others.

Information card

_____ **(Parish name)**
Project H.E.A.L.
Homebound Encouraged through Assistance in Love
A Special Ministry of Care to Homebound Parishioners

Name of Parishioner_____

Date of Birth_____

Address_____

_____

Phone_____

Lives alone? Yes ❑   No ❑

If no, with whom does the person live?_____

Name of parish caregiver_____

Phone _____

• Please record the date of any visitations next to each month. Mark C. if you brought communion.

January_____   **July**_____

February_____   **August**_____

March_____   **September**_____

April_____   **October**_____

May_____   **November**_____

June_____   **December**_____

Has a priest visited this parishioner for the sacrament of reconciliation?

Yes ❑   No ❑   If yes, when?————————————————————

Has parishioner received the sacrament of anointing of the sick lately?

Yes ❑   No ❑   If yes, when?————————————————————

Please include any other information that would be helpful in our ministry of care for this parishioner.

_____

_____

_____

CHAPTER NINE

Concluding Comments

As Christians, we are called by God to bind up the wounds of sick and elderly brothers and sisters as Christ did, bringing them healing hope and assurance by our loving solicitude and compassionate endeavors. Through a parish outreach such as Project H.E.A.L., it is possible to achieve these goals.

Healing power cannot be measured in words, but the blessings and benefits that flow from a ministry rendered in loving care, clearly manifest experiences of healing. In the following accounts of involvement with sick and elderly parishioners, although the environment and nature of their illnesses differ, each story speaks of a personal struggle in the midst of pain, and each ends with healing.

A telephone call from a neighbor alerted us about Rose, a parishioner in her eighties who lived alone, not far from her parish church. At one time, she was actively involved in her church, but when her arthritis worsened and her vision dimmed, she was no longer able to attend church and became lonely and depressed. A member of the parish ministry of care visited her, assessing her needs, gifting her with donations from the Parish Giving Tree, and adding her to our list for regular visitation. A phone call from Rose was followed by a note of gratitude expressing deep appreciation for her gifts and for being able to receive Holy Communion in her home on a regular basis. The depressed and sad tone in her voice lifted; this reflected a sign of healing hope.

Barbara had been skeptical about responding to the invitation to bring her mother, Helen, to the parish sacramental anointing of the sick. Because of her mother's acute stage of cancer, Barbara wanted to give her the opportunity to be anointed but wondered if efforts to transport her to the church would be worthwhile. She was concerned about Helen's inability to sit in the church pew and her lack of stamina to remain for the entire Mass. Barbara was assured that the parish team would readily assist by providing a special chair for her mother and by being there to help with any needs. Helen celebrated the sacrament of the anointing and managed to stay for the entire Mass. The singing at the Mass by the children brought her healing inspiration, and both Barbara and Helen were pleased to have participated in this liturgical celebration. Soon after this Eucharistic Liturgy, Barbara called to acknowledge how pleased her mother was to have been there and how tranquil she had become after receiving the sacrament despite the progression of her cancer. She had gained healing strength and freedom to surrender her sufferings to God. A few months later, Barbara informed us of her mother's peaceful death and of her repeated expressions of gratitude for the healing grace she had received through the sacrament of the anointing when she attended the communal service in the parish church.

John, age 31, was dying of AIDS in a local hospital. He was known by the medical staff for his unruly behavior, outrageous anger, and cantankerous moods. When anyone attempted to pay him a visit, they were cautioned about his unpredictable outbursts and was asked to leave the door of his room partly open, should his behavior cause someone harm.

When I approached John during a pastoral visit, his eyes widened, and the expression on his face revealed that he was under tremendous strain. I asked him if he would like me to read some of my prayer poems. He nodded in agreement, and in a distinct voice, said, "Yes, but would you please hold my hand." His right hand was bruised and clammy, and I gently held it as I read from the prayer cards. A transforming calm came over John's face after each prayer. He was no longer agitated and I had no reason to alert the nurses of any outburst. He remained pensive and quiet when I left his bedside. I learned later that John died peacefully not long after our encounter. He experienced a healing liberation. His words continue to ring in my ears as I ponder the effects of a compassionate touch. I often wonder if John's defiant behavior was the result of unexpressed fear or of the desperate need to feel the touch of someone's caring hand.

Elsie was in her nineties and lived alone. We frequently called to check on her and to inquire about her shopping needs. One day, during a regular call, there was a quiver in her voice. She had fallen on the floor from her bed and could not get up but managed to stretch far enough to answer the telephone ring. We dialed 911 for assistance, and soon after the ambulance personnel arrived at her home and transported her to the hospital. The results of a series of neurological tests confirmed that Elsie could no longer live at home alone. She was brought to a nursing home. We continued to stay in touch with her. She often wondered what would have happened to her, had we not made the telephone call to her that day, and admitted that the connection was definitely a healing moment in her life

Each of these accounts manifests a healing experience and shows how the individual shut-ins were encouraged through assistance in love as a result of a caring relationship.

The healing presence of Christ in us

Establishing a caring relationship between the giver and the receiver is a feature in parish ministry which cannot be overly emphasized. In a sense, it shows what it means to be another Simon of Cyrene or Veronica. To be in a caring relationship implies that someone embraces his or her own humanity and then comes forth in faith and courage to help another person carrying a cross. It means that someone freely brings relief to another by gently wiping the sweat off a brow when perhaps his or her own face is pain-ridden. It is what Jesus taught us to do during his public ministry when he went about healing bodies, minds, and spirits.

Cardinal Suenens once said, "Christ came not to take away our suffering, but to fill it with his presence." In the apostolic letter of Pope John Paul II, *On the Christian Meaning of Human Suffering*, we read: "Suffering cannot be transformed and changed by grace from outside but from within. And Christ through his own salvific suffering is very much present in every human suffering, and can act from within that suffering by the powers of his Spirit of truth, his consoling Spirit."

The parable of the Good Samaritan reminds us to apply the gospel of suffering, about which John Paul II speaks, in our encounters with others who may be experiencing some form of suffering. We must never "pass by on the other side indifferently; we must stop beside him. Everyone who stops beside the suffering of another person, whatever form it may take, is a Good Samaritan" (*On the Christian Meaning of Human Suffering*).

The expansion of a parish ministry of care acknowledges a special reaching out to the sick and elderly in a way that may not take away their suffering, but assuredly brings God's loving presence to them. Such a ministry allows them to experience renewed hope and healing care. This is the goal of Project H.E.A.L. and the motivational force behind every person who renders service in a parish outreach to its sick, disabled and elderly members.

As Pope John Paul II stated, "The name Good Samaritan fits every individual who is sensitive to the sufferings of others, who is moved by the misfortune of another."

Praise God for the many "Good Samaritans" who, through a parish ministry of care, are willing to take the time to "stop" beside their sick and elderly parishioners to encourage them, to pray with them, and to assist them while they are shut inside their homes or health care institutions and shut outside of their parish and community circles. May these dedicated volunteers reap copious blessings and inspire others to do the same in the name of Christ!

Resources

Books

Arnold, William and Margaret Fohl. *Christians and the Art of Caring*. Louisville, KY: John Knox/Westminster Press, 1988.

Barron, Robert. *The Strangest Way: Walking the Christian Path*. Maryknoll, NY: Orbis Books, 2002.

Bass, Dorothy C. *Practicing Our Faith*. San Francisco: Jossey-Bass Pub., 1998.

Bauer, Cecile. *Caregiver's Gethsemane: When a Loved One Longs to Die*. New York: Paulist Press, 1995.

Bosco, Antoinette. *The Pummeled Heart: Finding Peace through Pain*. Mystic, CT: Twenty-Third Publications, 1994.

Cain, Kenneth W. and Kaufman, Brian P. *Prayer, Faith and Healing*. Emmaus, PA: Rodale Press, 1999.

Callahan, Rachel and Rea McDonnell. *Harvest Us Home: Good News as We Age*. Cincinnati, OH: St. Anthony Messenger Press, 2000.

Champlin, Joseph M. and Taylor, Susan Champlin. *A Thoughtful Word, A Healing Touch*. Mystic, CT: Twenty-Third Publications, 1995.

Chapman, John H. *Facing Death: Stories of Spiritual Response to Serious Illness*. Chicago: ACTA Publications, 1998.

DeGidio, Sandra. *Prayer Services for the Elderly*. Mystic, CT: Twenty-Third Publications, 1996.

DeGrandis, Robert. *The Healing Ministry*. Lowell, MA: H.O.M. Books, 1985.

Department of Social Services, Elderly Service Division. *Health Ministry Partnership*. Meriden, CT: Department of Social Services, 1999.

Dossey, Larry. *Healing Words*. New York: Harper Collins Publishers, 1993.

———. *Prayer is Good Medicine*. San Francisco: Harper Publishers, 1996.

Feldmann, Robert M. *Friendly Visitors Training and Resource Manual*, first edition. Hartford, CT: Breakthrough to the Aging, 1996

Fisher, Bob. *Caring for a Dying Loved One*. New York: Alba House, 2001.

Fryer, Jane. *Living with Chronic Pain*. St. Louis, MO: Concordia, 1993.

Gallagher, Sr. Vera. "Healed by Prayer," *Catholic Digest*, June, 1997. Mystic, CT: Bayard Publications.

Gilbert, Richard. *Finding Your Way after Your Parent Dies*. Notre Dame, IN: Ave Maria Press, 1999.

Gordon, Beverly S. *Toward Peace: Prayer for the Widowed*. Cincinnati, OH: St. Anthony Messenger Press, 1990.

Groves, Richard. *The Sacred Art of Dying*. Cincinnati, OH: St. Anthony Messenger Press, 2000.

Gusmer, Charles W. *And You Visited Me: Sacramental Ministry to the Sick and Dying*. New York: Pueblo Publishing Co., 1989.

Hartman, Thomas. *Just a Moment*. Liguori, Missouri: Triumph Books, 1993.

Hill, Nancy. *Living with Terminal Illness*. St. Louis, MO: Concordia, 1995.

Hoagland, Victor. *Companion in Illness*. New York: Catholic Book Publishers, 1994.

Houts, Peter and Julia Bucher (project directors). *Prepared Family Caregivers Course*. Philadelphia, PA: Pennsylvania State University College of Medicine, 1999.

Hutchinson, Joyce and Joyce Rupp. *May I Walk You Home: Courage and Comfort for Caregivers of the Very Ill*. Notre Dame, IN Ave Maria Press, 1999.

Hynes, Millie. *The Ministry to the Aging*. Collegeville, MN: The Liturgical Press, 1989.

International Committee on English in the Liturgy. *Rite of Anointing and Pastoral Care of the Sick*. Collegeville, MN: The Liturgical Press, 1974.

———. *Pastoral Care of the Sick*. Collegeville, MN: The Liturgical Press, 1984.

John Paul II. *Letter of His Holiness to the Elderly*. Boston: Pauline Books and Media, 2000.

———. *On the Christian Meaning of Human Suffering*. Boston: Pauline Books and Media, 1984.

Kehrwald, Leif. *Caring that Enables*. New York: Paulist Press, 1991.

———. *Keeping in Touch with Parish Ministers Handbook*. Linden, NJ: Journal Press Resources, 1996.

Kofler, Marilyn, and O'Connor, Kevin. *Ministries of Care*. Chicago: Liturgy Training Publications, 1987.

Mace, Nancy L.and Rabins, Peter. *The 36-Hour Day*. Baltimore: The John Hopkins University Press, 1991.

Marsch, Michael. *Healing Through the Sacraments*. Collegeville, MN: The Liturgical Press, 1989.

Meredith, Owen. *Parish Activities Handbook*. Mystic, CT: Twenty-Third Publications, 1996.

Messer, Donald E. *Contemporary Images of Christian Ministry*. Nashville, TN: Abingdon Press, 1989.

Maxwell, Katie. *Bedside Manners*. Michigan: Barker Book House, 1990.

Miller, James E. *When You're the Caregiver*. Fort Wayne, IN: Willogreen Publishing Co., 1995.

Miller, Kent C. *Ministry to the Homebound*. San Jose, CA: Resource Publications, 1995.

Montongne, Martin. *Helping Others Cope with Illness at Home: Practical and Spiritual Applications*. Hartford, CT: Pastoral Services of Hartford Hospital, 1999.

Normile, Patti. *Prayer for Caregivers*. Cincinnati, OH: St. Anthony Messenger Press, 1995.

Office for Church Life and Leadership, United Church of Christ. *Called to Care: A Notebook for Lay Caregivers*. Berea, OH: United Church of Christ Resources, Inc., 1998.

Overberg, Kenneth R. *Into the Abyss of Suffering: A Catholic View*. Cincinnati, OH: St. Anthony Messenger Press, 2003.

Peel, Donald. *The Ministry of Listening*. Toronto, Canada: Anglican Book Centre, 1980.

Pontifical Council for the Laity. *The Dignity of Older People and their Mission in the Church and in the World*. Boston: Pauline Books and Media, 1999.

Ruane, Gerald. *Overcome Obstacles to Healing*. Caldwell, NJ: Sacred Heart Press, 1985.

Rupp, Joyce. *Praying Our Goodbyes*. Notre Dame, Indiana: Ave Maria Press, 1988.

———. *Your Sorrow Is My Sorrow: Hope and Strength in Times of Suffering*. New York: The Crossroad Publishing Co., 1999.

Roccapriore, Sr. Marie. *Anointing of the Sick and the Elderly: A Pastoral Guide for Home and Church*. Canfield, OH: Alba Books, 1980.

Schultz, Karl A. *The Art and Vocation of Caring for People in Pain*. New York: Paulist Press, 1993.

Shaw, Joan. *The Joy of Music in Maturity*. St. Louis, MO: MMB Music, Inc., 1997.

Stephen Leader's Training Course. *Christ Caring for People through People*. St. Louis, MO Stephen Ministries, 1999.

Strong, George. *Pastoral Care Among the Very Elderly* (D.Min.project). Hartford, CT: Hartford Seminary, 1985.

Simundson, Daniel J. *Faith Under Fire*. New York: Harper, 1991.

Thibeault, Edward. *Overcoming the Fear of Death*. Ijamsville, MD: Word Among Us Press, 1999.

Thomas, Leo and Alkire, Jane. *Healing as a Parish Ministry*. Notre Dame, IN: Ave Maria Press, 1992.

Thrash, Sara A. *Compassionate Caring for the Sick and Dying*. Mystic, CT: Twenty-Third Publications, 2000.

Vendura, Nancy. *Go! Do the Same*. New York: Paulist Press, 1992.

Walsh, Mary Paula. *Living After a Death*. Chicago: Veritas Publishing, 2000.

Articles and Pamphlets

Caron, Judith A. *Helps for Visiting the Sick*. Liguori, MO: Liguori, 1988.

Catholic Conference. *Administration of Communion and Viaticum to the Sick by an Extraordinary Minister*. Washington, D.C.: U.S. Conference of Catholic Bishops Publications Office, 1976.

Drahos, Mary. "Loving with a Disability." *New Covenant Magazine*. Huntington, IN: Our Sunday Visitor, June, 1997.

Episcopal Commission on Health Care. *Holistic Prescriptions* (newsletter). Philippines: Catholic Bishops Conference, 1997.

Fleo, Beatrice, ed. *Eucharistic Minister* (monthly newsletter). Kansas City, MO: National Catholic Reporter Publishing Company, Sept.,1999.

Families Who Care for Older Relatives. Wallingford, CT: Blue Cross/Blue Shield of Connecticut, 1990.

International Commission on English in the Liturgy. *Pastoral Care of the Sick and Dying: Study Text Revised Edition*. Washington, DC: U.S.C.C.B. Publications Office, 1984.

Interpretation: A Journal of Bible and Theology. "Salvation and Healing." Virginia: Union Theological Seminary, 1995.

Liturgy Documentary: Series 3, Pastoral Care of the Sick. Washington, D.C.: U.S.C.C.B. Office of Publications, 1983.

Lord, Janice Harris. *Being a Friend to Someone Who Hurts*. Meinrad, IN: Abbey Press, 1990.

Murray, Rev. Albert A. *Bedside Prayers*. Meinrad, IN: Abbey Press, 1995.

Myers, Kenneth. "The Art of Suffering: It's Not a Matter of Killing Pain but of Using it Right," in *New Covenant* magazine, February 1999. Huntington, IN: Our Sunday Visitor, Inc.

Pastoral Care Week. (packet). St. Louis MO: Council on M.S.S., 1999.

Patterson, Rev. Robert A. *Pastoral Health Care: Understanding the Church's Healing*. St. Louis, MO: Catholic Health Association of U.S., 1983.

Peale, Norman V. "Learning to Pray" from *In God's Hands*. Excerpt in *Woman's Day* magazine, April 20, 1999.

Ponder, Eileen. "Communion of the Sick and Homebound," in *Eucharistic Ministries* newsletter, August 2003. Kansas City, MO: National Catholic Reporter.

Richstatter, Thomas. *Would You Like to be Anointed?* Cincinnati, OH: Saint Anthony Messenger Press, 1987.

Rudolph, Laura A. *When Your Brother or Sister Has Cancer*. New York: American Cancer Society, 1984.

Scott, Robert Owens, ed. *Spirituality and Health*. New York: Spirituality and Health Publishing Company, Fall, 1999.

Audiocassettes

Burke, William. *A Spirituality for Depression*. Cincinnati, OH: St. Anthony Messenger Press, 2001.

DeGrandis, Robert. *Healing Power of Prayer*. Albuquerque, NM: Hand Productions, 1998.

Gusmer, Charles. *Rite of Anointing and Pastoral Care of the Sick*. Kansas City, MO: NCR Cassettes, 1978.

Johnson, Elizabeth. *Suffering and Catholic Tradition*. Cincinnati, OH: St. Anthony Messenger Press, 1996.

Normile, Patti. *Visiting the Sick*. Cincinnati, OH: St. Anthony Messenger Press, 1997.

Riley, Carole. *How to be a Prayer Partner*. Cincinnati, OH: St. Anthony Messenger Press, 1998.

Willig, Jim and Tammy Bundy. *Lessons from the School of Suffering*. Cincinnati, OH: St. Anthony Messenger Press, 2003.